The Pocket Essential

VIDEOGAMING

www.pocketessentials.com

First published in Great Britain 2003 by
Pocket Essentials, P O Box 394, Harpenden, Herts, AL5 1XJ, UK

Distributed in the USA by Trafalgar Square Publishing,
PO Box 257, Howe Hill Road, North Pomfret, Vermont 05053

A CIP catalogue record for this book is available from the British Library.

ISBN 1-904048-20-X

2 4 6 8 10 9 7 5 3 1

Book typeset by Wordsmith Solutions Ltd
Printed and bound by Cox & Wyman

CONTENTS

Introduction

With the millennium now past, an entire generation that does not know life without computers has been born. In the past forty years we have seen huge technological leaps: computers, the Internet, and mobile phones, among many other fantastic things. The human nature to 'play' and have fun somehow mingled with these technologies, and somehow videogames were the result. Many may remember the first time they experienced the sights, sounds and frantic action of their first arcade game, but there are now many more who find picking up a controller and jumping through pixellated imaginary worlds as second nature as holding a pencil.

The history of videogames has certainly been a rocky road. It took a while to find the right game to catch the public's attention, but when they were interested they were hooked, desperate for the latest games. Videogames have even survived economic setbacks, refusing to be destroyed by a fickle market, always managing to evolve into something new to capture the imagination and find some way to invade lives and homes. And as time has gone on the culture has grown and split; videogaming is no longer a quick pastime to some, it is a hobby, an obsession, a career, even. This popularity has lead to a permeation of popular culture: character names and company brands are well known in the home and on the high street. But at the same time, this newly emerged media has come under attack for being dangerous and bad for the mind by a tabloid press possibly looking for somewhere to point the finger. Videogaming. It's the new rock 'n' roll.

It is a very stringent media. Games are only remembered if they are of a great quality. The bad fall to the wayside, and the good mould the future. *Pong*, *Manic Miner*, *The Legend of Zelda* all have a special something. The design, the controls, and the content are placed in a clever mix that cannot be found in any other media. At the same time it is wrapped in a careful technological blanket, still changing, still finding new ways to entertain. We like to wrap ourselves in this blanket, buying into each successive hardware generation, watching on as the marketing men try to outdo each other, making our choice and voting with our wallets.

Carry on reading to find out about the history of gaming, the best games produced, and aspects of videogaming culture. We love games. We hope you do too.

History

The Origins (Pre-1972)

Founding Fathers

For some gamers, it is inconceivable to imagine a time when videogames did not exist. Yet, pre-1970s, they may as well not have. It is ironic now that out of all the staple 'leisure' activities, videogaming has become one of the fastest growing and most lucrative. In the stretch of decades that predated the birth of videogames, many companies were established that would later be major forces in the world of electronic entertainment. Many new technologies ere invented, and many people took jobs that would secure their place as leading figures in an industry that would grow and grow (and at times crash and burn).

A recurring theme in the origins of videogames is that a lot of developments relied on enterprising Americans. As with other cultural phenomena, the efforts of this small handful of individuals would snowball into a far greater force than was originally conceived. In 1952, a man called David Rosen started a moderate import business in Japan. Rosen Enterprises imported all kinds of goods to Japan, which was recovering economically after the events of World War Two. Among the things Rosen imported were American photo booths and coin operated mechanical games. His trade was so successful that he managed to acquire manufacture companies, which produced the likes of games and jukeboxes, whose products he could sell in both America and Japan. Rosen's company merged with that of some other importers, called Service Games, abbreviated to Sega. They became renowned for the various machines they introduced to Japan, with mechanical games a speciality. They also became known for producing and distributing one-arm bandits in other territories of the world.

In 1958, William Higinbotham devised what is arguably the first kind of electronic interactive game at Brookhaven National Laboratory, in the USA. Aware that visitors to his laboratory were bored by static displays, he and colleague Robert Dvorak modified an oscillator to play a simple tennis game called *Tennis For Two*. The game offered a side-on view of a tennis court, and two players used a dial and a button to control the trajectory of the ball's movement and had to correctly time their striking of the ball back across the court. *Tennis For Two* was powered by the computers and machines used to analyse and predict missile trajectories during World War Two merely modified for fun. However the game's existence was a very isolated incident; only those visiting the laboratory came into contact with it, and it is most unlikely that the game had any bearings on the similar games that were to appear in the future.

The 1960s were exciting times for those at the Massachusetts Institute for Technology (MIT); those students luckily enough to be admitted were allowed to work on some of the most powerful computing machines of the time. For one group of students, the Tech Model Railroad Club, this was somewhat a dream come true: they endlessly discussed works of science fiction and often made up many science fiction scenarios of their own. The MIT computer mainframes were massive and were often set up with very rudimentary electronic game displays (mazes, bouncing ball simulations) in order to show the public what they were capable of. The machines were gradually updated with more powerful units, and in 1961 it was decided that a far more taxing game demonstration be created for their new machine, the PDP-1.

Spacewar! was created by Steve Russell, helped by fellow TMRC members and other computer 'hackers' (the phrase was coined at MIT). The original mandate was to create something that would engage the player and show the full power and capabilities of the PDP-1. The result more than filled this aim, offering a space combat game, wherein two players fought against each other using either a wedge- or needle-shaped spacecraft. *Spacewar!*'s concept was not patented and thus many games have since borrowed from the concept behind it; most notably in videogaming's immediate future were the likes of *Computer Space*, *Asteroids*, and *Space Invaders*. The game was much perfected by Russell and company, culminating in the addition of skill levels and non-player objects (a star in the middle of the playing field acted as an obstacle that needed avoiding). Most notably the game was the first to have a specially made controller that, while very basic, offered all the controls needed to play the game, using sticks to control speed and movement.

Spacewar! was a cultural item akin to *Tennis For Two*; it was not available to everybody, and was ultimately forgotten by many. Unlike *Tennis For Two*, however, it was not forgotten by everyone. *Spacewar!*, available to other universities with computing departments, was hosted on the University of Utah's PDP-1 machine, where student Nolan Bushnell became obsessed with it. His love of the game would shape his career. Bushnell had faith that the game would appeal to many if given the right backing, and he set about turning the concept into a mass-market coin operated game. The idea didn't come to fruition until he graduated in 1970, when he met Ted Dabney, who also believed that *Spacewar!* was marketable. In 1971, Nutting Associates, who manufactured electronic coin-up trivia games for bars, decided to buy and distribute Bushnell's version of *Spacewar!*, called *Computer Space*.

1,500 *Computer Space* units were made. The game's cabinet had a distinctive fibreglass shell, with a small control panel and an adequate screen displaying scores. But it wasn't a success. The game failed to spark any real interest, or generate large profits, most likely because of the over-complicated controls that put new players at a disadvantage. Plus, most of the prospective players were half-drunk barflies; getting them interested in anything more complicated than a darts board was a challenge. Bushnell and Dabney made only $500.

Five years before *Computer Space*, however, an attempt to take electronic entertainment into the home was embarked upon, and while it did not come to fruition until 1972, after *Computer Space*'s failure, it was moderately successful. In 1966, television engineer Ralph Baer began work with military contractor Sanders Associates. For some time Baer had been mulling over his thoughts on the passivity of television, and wanted to devise something that was interactive. Working with some colleagues, the Home TV Game was born. Top brass at Sanders gave Baer permission to work on the device full time, and the eventual outcome was a unit that plugged into the TV, capable of displaying a ping-pong game and variants upon it. While Baer was successful in patenting this original device in 1968, Sanders Associates lost interest, and the project was to be cancelled.

Baer was not put off by this rebuff, and he approached other TV manufacturers with his ideas for home entertainment, yet most were not interested. He did, however, catch the eye of Bill Benders, who pursued the project once he had moved to a senior position at Magnavox. Demonstrations helped Benders and Baer win over the rest of the executives at Magnavox, and the decision to license the Home TV Game and its patents was made.

Released in September 1972, the result was the Magnavox *Odyssey*, the first games console available to the public. It was priced at $100 and sold 100,000 units. It was a moderate success, and real value for money; the console came with over 300 separate pieces, including toy money, counters, and plastic overlays to place over the screen to liven up rudimentary graphics. The unit was primitive and unwieldy, but the pack of bits 'n' pieces offered a variety of gameplay. The Odyssey was more a hybrid of home board games and electronic entertainment than an actual videogame in its own right, but it prepared the public for the phenomenon that was to emerge later that year.

It is hard to believe that a unit requiring so much work from the user could spark off the phenomenon that has lasted thirty years, yet the meagre beginnings of the Odyssey were nothing compared to what was about to happen later in 1972.

'The Golden Age' (1972-81)

'AVOID MISSING BALL FOR HIGH SCORE'

To promote the Odyssey, Magnavox took a roadshow around America. Visitors were allowed to experience the console and its games first hand. One of those visitors was none other than Nolan Bushnell.

Bushnell had parted company with Nutting Associates, and he and Dabney had started a games company of their own, using their $500 profit from *Computer Space*. The company was called Atari. Bushnell was inspired by a simplistic tennis game running on Baer's machine and decided to use a similar idea as a way to break open the games market. Al Alcorn was hired to create Atari's first game—Bushnell encouraged Alcorn along by claiming they had business deals to support manufacture—and the product of Alcorn's work was *Pong*.

Pong was a two-player game; each player used a small dial to move a paddle up and down on the screen. Bushnell never thought much of the game, seeing it as a stepping-stone to greater things. He took the game to various manufacturers, all of whom turned it down. Bushnell was undeterred at proving the worth of electronic games, and decided to prove their viability himself. He took the game to the Andy Capps tavern in Sunnyvale, California, and did a deal to leave it running there for a week. (It was set up in a cabinet like *Computer Space*, and accepted quarters to allow play.)

Myth says that the Andy Capps' manager had to call Bushnell a week later demanding he remove the machine as it had broken and wasn't pulling any customers. This is not completely true. He did call Bushnell, but to inform him that it needed fixing and fast because of the customer demand. Bushnell investigated the fault. It was jammed full of quarters. Bushnell decided that Atari should manufacture their own *Pong* machines. This was the risk-taking decision that finally blew the videogames market wide open.

The Arcade Age

Atari hired more people in order to roll out the *Pong* machines, and Bushnell's original hunch that the market was ripe for such a game was proven correct. The success of *Pong* was phenomenal; they sold 8,000 machines, and in 1973 they made $3.2million.

The success of *Pong* kept other companies afloat too. A slew of copycat machines appeared that year, notable not by the quality of the game, but in their quantity, with countless companies all releasing numerous variants on the same idea. But these copycats weren't the only guilty parties; Atari too

11

made variants of their *Pong* idea, adding obstacles and different arena designs. Imitation may well be the highest form of flattery, but this is a type of derivative, copy-cat behaviour that would recur in the industry. The explosion of the market had somewhat frightened Ted Dabney, who sold his half of Atari to Bushnell.

Atari had sparked something off with *Pong*, but they also needed to prove their worth. They did this in 1974 with a game called *Tank*. Back in the pinball era, distributors demanded sole rights to a manufacturer's games, but Atari were wary of letting this happen with their products, so they set up a secret subsidiary called Kee Games to make sure that at least some of their games had better distribution deals. The game itself featured a maze that one or two players had to navigate; *Tank* was a technological leap, using read only memory (ROM) chips to store graphics; the days of *Pong*'s simple graphics were already old news. The game went on to be the most popular arcade game that year.

The arcade boom was on, and while Atari had claimed a firm place in this snowballing element of popular culture, many other companies were also making headways with creative new games for the new technology. More and more arcade games were popping up in bars, bowling alleys and pinball dens around America, and soon became reliable money-spinners.

Home Space, Invaded

Since the failure of the Odyssey, the home market had been overlooked, but ignorance of this market wasn't going to last: various companies would soon learn that it was the most profitable area to make games for, especially Atari, who would come to rely upon it.

In 1975 Atari produced a home version of *Pong*. This was a unit with two paddles built in which could be hooked up to a TV. It took a battle to get the product out to the public (it was finished in 1974) but retailers were at first reticent, despite the success of the arcade version, because of the short life of the Odyssey. A deal was done with the department store Sears; they would be exclusive stockists, the game would be marketed under their own 'Tele-Games' label, and they would advertise it. The success was so far unprecedented, with eventual sales of 150,000 units. Again, Atari's device was mimicked by a slew of electronics companies, but this version of *Pong* triggered another trend in videogaming; that of demand being so high, customers were prepared to queue up for hours to get their hands on a unit.

Atari had to take a $10million credit agreement to meet Sears' production demands, but this didn't matter; by the end of 1975 they were making $40 million in sales. They had become a successful market player, firmly supplanting the notion of electronic gaming into the national consciousness. In 1976, Warner Communications bought Atari for $28 million, with Bushnell making £16million and being made CEO. Videogaming had finally arrived, corporate style.

As soon as Warner had taken over Atari, the company set to work on a secret project, codenamed Stella. The device was a home machine, which would use programmable cartridges to store games on. The console, the Video Computer System (VCS) was launched in 1977, just before Christmas, but wasn't the instant success that Warner or Atari were hoping for. While it came with a supplied game, and was at an acceptable price of $250, it didn't immediately catch on the way home *Pong* had. Warner's stock market value was falling, and in 1978 Bushnell left Atari. With Bushnell out of the way, Atari changed internally. An idea to replicate the booming arcade experience in the home was hit upon, and this was the decision that reversed the fortunes of the VCS. A deal to make a home version of the popular *Space Invaders* was secured, and Atari became the first company to license arcade games; the release of *Space Invaders* in 1980 made the company $100 million.

From 1980-82, the VCS was the doyenne of home videogaming. 25 million VCSs are sold, netting Atari $5 billion; 200 games are created for the system, by 40 manufactures, selling 120 million cartridges; given that Atari made a profit from all cartridges sold, during this period they were responsible for almost half of Warner's profits.

Other Contenders

Many other companies were keen to have machines in this profitable market, and the rest of the period was littered with the launches of other home consoles. Some were moderately successful; others were small blips on the radar of videogaming.

First up, was the Fairchild Channel F, launched in 1976. It was the first of the home consoles to use pre-programmed cartridges (the Odyssey's 'cartridges' were more units that completed the circuit running through the device). The major flaw for the Channel F was that by the time of its launch, the games and graphics seemed out of date.

The Bally Professional Arcade was an example of a manufacturer slightly misinterpreting the market. Launched in 1978, the console was admirable for its mix of education (the system featured built in calculator and art 'games') and fun. The machine had superior controllers, and it was essentially the first home machine to allow play for four players. But $300 was too expensive for consumers and eventually Bally abandoned the machine.

The Odyssey also refused to accept its fate as one of videogaming's losers. In 1974, Magnavox were subsidised by Philips, who later decided to re-release the machine on the back of the current videogame boom. The result was 1978's Odyssey^2. The machine was an erratic mess in so many ways. Despite boasting some built-in games, a powerful processor and a keyboard, the unit's graphics were really no better than the original Odyssey; the joy-sticks were hardwired into the boards (so, if one of the controllers broke, there was no way to replace them save returning the entire machine); most terribly, the machine was only available in the US via specialist Magnavox dealers. The machine was a moderate success in Europe, and was eventually re-released there with a monitor and peripherals. Just over one million Odyssey^2 units were sold, but this was nowhere near enough to compete with the VCS.

Mattel's Intellivision (an abbreviation of Intelligent Television) was launched across the US in 1980. The console, boasting a 16-bit processor (beating the likes of Sega by almost ten years), was the most capable of all the challengers to the VCS; it was graphically superior, with a good selection of games, and one million were sold during 1982-83. This does coincide with the growing disenfranchisement of the Atari consumer, but seeing as the sales go against the dip in market value of the time, they are quite an achievement.

But there was trouble on the horizon; as well as the oncoming 'great crash', Mattel were also forced to pay Magnavox million dollar fees for utilis-ing similar technologies to their home console devices. No such action was taken against Atari as they had already made licensing payments to secure their machine's place on the market. Also, Mattel's attempts to use the device as a bridge between home consoles and home computing meant they spread themselves too thin: a long promised keyboard for the main unit was a major disappointment, and follow up machines, the Intellivision II and III were tech-nological steps down the evolutionary ladder, with programmers suggesting that the new machines were relics of the 70s.

Most interesting was the Vectrex. Offering parents a solution to single-tele-vision households, the machine boasted a built-in screen, a design element that arose solely because designer Jay Smith had to find a use for some sur-plus vector monitors. The machine launched in 1982, unfortunately coincid-ing with the oncoming 'crash' in the market. However, because the device offered something new, and allowed some parents the chance to reclaim their TV, it was surprisingly popular for a while. Milton Bradley bought manufac-turer General Consumer Electronics, but when the vector monitors ran out, and consumer interest waned throughout 1982-83; production costs meant MB had to abandon the device.

The Atari Age

These contenders never managed to achieve the brand recognition or market penetration Atari had. Not enough consumers were willing to turn away from the all-American company they had already invested in and which was in so many ways solely responsible for the mass-market gaming trend. The VCS, with its huge library of games, and solid support from all sectors was the only real machine of choice for the era.

The world of videogaming, and Atari's grip on it, had snowballed, but that snowball was going to melt; from 1982, the industry was becoming a tougher place to survive in…

The End? (1982-84)

Game Over

The word 'boom' doesn't really cover the extent to which the videogame medium had affected the decade of years prior to 1982. Arcades were running a buzzing trade from the new electronic games; Atari was a household name, and numerous games characters were iconic, all with spin off merchandise; many other companies were trying to contest the VCS's grip on the market. But the home entertainment marketplace wasn't going to survive when placed under such weight.

Atari were keen to maintain their lead in the market, but things were going to take a turn for the worst. The company had changed a great deal from the communal atmosphere of 1972 to the corporate one of 1982. Decisions were made executively, based on sales and money, rather than the passionate quality-focused efforts that came from the company in the 70s.

Pac-Man was a huge hit in the arcade, and Atari quickly purchased the licence from Namco, wanting to get a VCS version in the shops ASAP. The cartridge appeared in 1982, and went on to become one of the biggest selling games of the era, all due to the name of the licence and the time of launch. The game was, however, rubbish. Poorly implemented with shoddy design, it couldn't even be classed a poor relative of its arcade brethren because it was so clearly a rush job.

Greed was saturating the US market—every conceivable licence had a game made for it and the result was a period in videogaming where the proportion of awful output outweighed the good; the market could not cope with this kind of overload. And Atari wasn't just responsible for the lacklustre *Pac-Man* game, they were about to make another big mistake.

Another game rushed out in 1982 was a tie-in to the blockbuster movie *E.T.* (then the highest grossing movie of all time). Atari paid $21 million to get the licence for the game and, as with their *Pac-Man* clone, rushed the VCS game into production. It showed. But the poor gameplay mechanics were not just what this game would be famous for. Atari were convinced that the game would be as successful as the film, and mindlessly produced five million cartridges; more than the actual number of VCS machines in circulation. Eventually, only one million units would sell: a disaster. Atari were left with one of the biggest flops of the time.

1982 also saw the launch of more new consoles, with even more companies vying for a slice of the home entertainment pie. That year saw Atari release the successor to the VCS, the Atari 5200. The launch was spectacularly uneven; the machine, while more powerful than its predecessor, offered a line-up of games that couldn't compare to the breadth of titles for the VCS, or even compete with the current offering from the likes of Mattel and Coleco. Generally, the machine smacked of poor effort (most memorable was the terrible joystick on offer).

Also in 1982, the Colecovision appeared, and like the Odyssey and Intellivision, it made attempts to bridge the gap between console and computer in order to grab the market's attention, but like the Vectrex its launch unfortunately coincided with the oncoming dip in consumer interest. Made by Coleco Indsutries, the machine was designed as a way to remain in the previously booming home entertainment market and also recoup the millions lost after flooding the market with countless *Pong* clones. The system debuted at a moderate $199, and boasted rather impressive graphical and audio capabilities. Following Atari's lead, Coleco made sure they had popular arcade games available for their machine. The main draw to the console at first was that Coleco had made a deal with Nintendo to offer the home version of *Donkey Kong* on their system, and another popular arcade game featured was *Zaxxon*. In 1983, the machine sold 1.5 million units, beating not only Mattel and the Intellivision, but also both Atari machines (the VCS and the new 5200).

Coleco ran into trouble when they tried to cross over to computing with their ADAM machine, a standalone console/computer. A ridiculously high price tag ($600) meant that the device was met with indifference from the public, who were already jaded by poor efforts from Atari. Plus, the ADAM hardware was full of technical bugs, and by 1984 Coleco has lost over $250 million. A drop in price did not help matters (in fact, it can be argued that price slashing makes consumers more wary); even profits from Coleco's other big money spinner, the Cabbage Patch Dolls, did not help their situation. Left with piles of unwanted machines, Coleco abandoned the machine in 1985.

A clear indication that things weren't going so well for Atari came at the end of December 1982, when they announced their projected profits for that year. Their estimate was at approximately 15 percent increase in sales, which shocked many; sources within the company were previously suggesting closer to fifty. Shareholders panicked, and the value of Warner Communications stock dramatically dropped within days. Financially, videogaming was perceived to be on the rocks.

Videogaming, after such a dramatic rise in popularity, was losing favour with the world. The customer had lost interest in normal video games, distracted by computing, and put off by the depths Atari and co. had plummeted to. There were too many consoles, and too many inadequate games and machines. By 1983 Atari warehouses were full of dead stock and unwanted inventory. In one of the most infamous occurrences in videogames history—and the most telling of decline—they decided to dump the surplus product (mainly *E.T.* cartridges) at a landfill site in New Mexico claiming it was defective stock. It was a poor attempt to bury their problems, but the one thing they wouldn't be able to dismiss away or bury was the lack of confidence in videogames, from the consumer, the retailers and the shareholders.

By 1984 the US videogame industry was a meagre shadow of its former self. In 1983, Atari lost so much money that their losses stood at $536million; they had lost money at a rate of $2million a day! The problems with home entertainment had a slight knock on to the arcades too: despite some quality titles still drawing in customers, takings practically halved, and many had to shut down.

Continue

To a great extent, however, one of the reasons for the downfall of the home console was also the same thing that was to sustain it throughout the slump: home computing. The use of microcomputers was on the rise, and was very much attracting customers away from the likes of Atari. Technology was on a continued progression but to an extent Atari had ignored this, sticking solely to cartridges (a similarly bad decision would be made by Nintendo almost fifteen years later). Meanwhile, other companies moved forward with using magnetic based media—disks and cassettes—that were capable of holding more information. The result allowed more powerful machines to be manufactured that were capable of offering more possibilities (as well as games they opened avenues for programming, home office use, etc.) and they soon found their way into the home in place of the standard games machine. Prime examples are the machines released by Commodore (the VIC-20 and the Commodore 64) and Sinclair (the Spectrum series).

Already in the home computer business, after the release of the Commodore PET machine in 1977, they decided that the way forward was with affordable home microcomputers. 1980's VIC-20 was that very device. Retailing at an amazingly cheap $300, it undercut the cost of its nearest rival by almost $200, and became the first home computer to sell one million units. It was the machine's simple technology build that meant it was cheap to produce and sell, but because of these restrictions it was calling out for a successor fairly quickly. That successor came in 1982, the Commodore 64. The C64 was an improved version of the VIC-20, with increased memory and a custom sound chip. In the US, Commodore had successfully taken on the Apple II computer and won: the C64 sold 22 million machines, and was the biggest selling computer of its kind.

In Britain, the C64 was famous in bedrooms and playgrounds as the enemy of the machines available from Sinclair Computers. Originally, the line of computers made available by Sinclair were kits to be constructed by the user, marketed to satisfy the curiosity of technobuffs who were tired of buying home-assembly radios, and also to fund more important Sinclair projects. Games came as an accident; the first of these kits, the ZX80, was capable of being programmed using BASIC (Beginners All-Purpose Symbolic Instruction Code), and it was in a guide to implementing that language on the machine that you could find instructions on programming simplistic games. What made the ZX series so popular was the price; in kit form, or pre-assembled, the early units were always at affordable prices under £100, unlike the Commodore or Atari home computers that were ridiculously expensive in comparison. Like the machines from Commodore, the Spectrum could read data stored magnetically on cassettes, using an add-on tape-reader. The rival computers had better graphics, sound, and memory capabilities, but this didn't deter users from the Sinclair products. By the end of 1981, 350,000 ZX81s had been sold (mainly in the UK), an impressive achievement given that the machine was only available via one high street retailer.

The ZX Spectrum followed in April 1982, and despite Sinclair's best efforts to market the machine as a business computer, younger users were obsessed with programming their own games; the Speccy, as it became known, was in great demand, and throughout the year supplies were always running out. At the same time, the C64 was launched, but with a steep £350 price tag. Throughout 1983, the Spectrum went from strength to strength, with sales in that year of 200,000 units; Sinclair Computers was making almost £14million in profits.

These microcomputers were successful in that they offered the arcade experience in the home; but they also allowed you to make your own games.

The machines offered a sense of empowerment to younger gamers, and could also be considered educational by parents or older gamers. Even though the likes of the C64 and the Spectrum were eventually outdone by newer, more powerful home computers, the mark they left on a generation of gamers remains indelible, as was its effect on games retail, cunningly offering gamers a route away from the dark period in home videogaming, but still managing to keep a love of games alive.

'The Great Video Games Crash' was very much limited to the US; it is worth remembering that in Europe and Japan the games industry continued practically unharmed by the American slump. Each territory had a reason for this: home computing was on the rise in Europe, thanks to Sinclair and Commodore, and the European territory merely made the transition from consoles to computing; and in Japan gaming was sustained by Sega and Nintendo. In fact, it was to be the last of the four that would see to the resurgence of videogames worldwide...

Extra Life (1985-88)

As the industry crashed around the ears of the American businessmen who had helped create and cultivate it, the story in Japan was different. Home gaming worldwide was still continuing, thanks to the popularity of microcomputers, but it was the Japanese and their consoles that were really going to kick things off again, thanks to Sega and Nintendo.

Nintendo's history of gaming stretches back much further than the import business started by David Rosen. 1889 saw the founding of Marufuku: they were a company aimed at producing playing cards, and by 1907 they adopted manufacture of Westernised playing cards as well. The product was hugely successful, and Marufuku eventually secured rights to use Disney and other marketable characters on their cards, guaranteeing more sales. In 1951, the company changed name to The Nintendo Playing Card Company, Nintendo meaning 'leave luck to the heavens.'

Nintendo had seen how forms of entertainment like bowling and arcades, had drawn in huge crowds, and by the 1970s were trying their hand at laser-based shooting range simulations, which failed to catch on. Meanwhile they dabbled with coin-op electronic games. Their efforts in the field were limited solely to Japan, but of a high quality; they were the first to greatly increase the graphical capability of arcade games by introducing microprocessors to the machines (1976) and previous to that had experimented with 16mm film and video techniques in order to enhance the games. Work culminated in 1979 with the opening of an operations division to deal with production of arcade games. Nintendo also tackled the home market, and in 1976 they licensed the Atari technology to create their own home *Pong* games, the Colour TV Game 6, followed by the Colour TV Game 15. In 1980 they branched out, announcing a new America-based subsidiary, Nintendo of America, Inc (NOA), located in New York. NOA would be responsible for importing and selling Japanese-made toys and games within the US. At first the company distributed the *Game & Watch* series, and later their eventually successful arcade games. So far, they had slowly expanded and consolidated, equally mimicking the market and supplying their own innovations.

Their tactics changed in 1983, however, with the Japanese launch of their home games machine, the Famicom (a contracted version of 'Family Computer'—a name that cunningly suggests a vast array of possibilities for a console). Despite licensing their biggest arcade hit (*Donkey Kong*) out to Coleco, they were not going to let the home market expand without them. The Famicom was another cartridge-based console, 8-bit power, and a low price (approximately $100) meant that Nintendo sold 500,000 units in Japan only two months after release. Nintendo produced all the games themselves, demonstrating a reasonably strong talent at making quality party games. However, Nintendo's success was briefly challenged when it emerged that some of the Famicoms were faulty. In order to counter bad press and discontent from customers, Nintendo recalled all the Famicoms and replaced the faulty chips as a safety measure; the gesture paid off, and customer confidence had been secured. Over the next year, Nintendo would sell another million of the units.

Still, the US industry was not interested in videogames. Nintendo tried to get Atari interested in licensing the Famicom, but because of the US slump, no deals were made. When Nintendo tried to take the machine to retailers themselves, they were left with cold shoulders from buyers unwilling to take a risk on the technology that was now so unfavourable. Nintendo were not going to be put off. Instead, they relied on their faith in the machine, and buoyed by the fact that arcades were still drawing a profit, Nintendo thought up a new approach.

For the market outside of Japan the Famicom was reborn as the NES: the Nintendo Entertainment System. The idea was to distance the machine from previous toys and games, trying instead to appeal to the serious nature that made home computers successful, implying an entertainment system that could offer many uses, much like the original 'Family Computer' name. Words like 'videogames' and 'cartridge' were to be avoided at all costs in marketing the machine in the US. Nintendo devised a light gun for the machine, sleek controllers, and the unit itself was turned into a grey box.

Despite what retailers were still telling them, Nintendo were confident, and decided to push the hard sell on the toughest market in the US, New York. 1985 saw Nintendo dispatch a team of salesmen to the city. The only way to get retailers interested was to offer them complete immunity should the machine fail to catch on. Nintendo would stock the store and set up displays; the retailers would rake in the profits in return for the shop floor space. Gradually, the idea won favour and almost 600 toy stores and electronics shops across New York took on the product, with Nintendo salesmen working right up to Christmas day. Nintendo's confidence flew against the continued reticence to place faith in anything videogame related, and it was proven correct: 50,000 NESs were sold that Christmas in New York—the next year, when the NES was rolled out nationally, a million units were sold. In 1987, three million were sold. Nintendo were well on the way to rebuilding the US home videogame market.

It was the quality of games, as well as the hardware, that was making sure people followed the NES. A robot (called ROB) was also designed and came with the first wave of NESs; it was a reason to buy the machine for parents and gamers, playing on the ideas of both entertainment and education. In truth, ROB was just a Trojan horse in order to get the machine into homes; it was the other games that Nintendo would secure users with. The zapper gun worked with *Duck Hunt* – rudimentary clay pigeon shooting, but near revolutionary to some home gamers – and another game packed in with the machine was *Super Mario Bros.*, featuring the iconic Mario in a near perfect conversion of the arcade game. In 1987, *The Legend of Zelda* sold one million copies, and climbing — it and *Mike Tyson's Punch Out* both eventually sold two million units. But it wasn't just the quality of software that ensured their success: the NES offered easier access to videogames, as opposed to the home computers which were seen as complicated to run, and thus it was a hit with children. Plus, Nintendo were the only real force on the market; no one else was willing to take the risk that people may still be interested in videogames, if tackled correctly, leaving Nintendo to seize the market.

In Europe, the NES didn't catch on as strongly; by 1992, after the launch of the SNES, the NES had sold a total of 3.5 million units. Not a disaster, given the machine was a worldwide success, but nowhere near on par with the Japanese and American territories. Uneven distribution and a choppy release schedule (something European Nintendo fans are forced to grumble about regardless of the hardware generation) meant that the machine got off to a slow start; Nintendo also had to cope with the popularity of the Spectrum and C64, and also the attempts by Sega to enter the 8-bit arena.

After the boom of the 70s, Sega had branched out into making their own arcade games; they had their own *Pong* clone, and soon branched out into original gaming. Sega's machines eventually made their way over to arcades in foreign shores, with quality titles like *Zaxxon* and *Frogger*, and large striking cabinets with unique features that always drew attention.

Sega had already lined up machines in the home videogame market in Japan. 1983 saw the launch of the SG-1000, their first videogame console. This was followed by the SC-3000, a console-cum-computer, with other peripherals available for both machines. The line of machines Sega introduced in Japan offered ports of some of their arcade classics, but to many extents these were just tests of what they could achieve, and their next project, the Sega Master System (SMS) seemed a far fuller concept.

The SMS had more memory, a better audio chip, and faster processor than the NES. It predominately played games from cartridges, but the original version of the console also had a slot for credit-card sized cards that could store games. Some hilarious-looking 3-D goggles were also designed in order to play games that ran from the cards in 3-D, however, the new storage format failed to catch on. Like the NES, a small rectangular controller was used, featuring a directional pad and A-B buttons. A light gun, the Light Phaser, was also available (similar to the NES' device, but actually of a higher quality). Strangely, the pause button was located on the base unit itself.

Having seen that Nintendo had successfully entered the US videogame market, Sega decided to try their hand at taking their videogames console worldwide, but launched months after the NES had established itself, in 1986, so it was never going to be a decent contender against it. Plus, it was slightly more expensive in the US than the NES ($200 as opposed to Nintendo's $159), and customers were more likely to veer towards the Nintendo product despite the Sega machines' few technical advantages. Too many people had already taken the NES as their machine of choice, and few were willing to give the new console a chance.

Much gets made of the fact that the SMS was supremely unpopular, and while it certainly never reached the heights of Nintendo's 8-bit glory, it is worth bearing in mind that it did have a solid user base throughout Europe and Australia, thanks to some solid software support in those territories. In America, however, the story was different. It is estimated that Nintendo held up to 90% of the videogames market, and the word 'Nintendo' was being used as a catchall phrase for all videogames. Sega of America, desperate to improve upon the disappointing SMS launch, sold distribution rights to Tonka, believing that the added impetus of the toy company would help boost sales. But decent distribution was the only advantage the deal with Tonka allowed, and

Tonka ignored those titles that were selling well in Europe and other territories, choosing instead to release games whose potential popularity was untested. Plus, Nintendo's hold on third party developers hardly helped Sega's machine. Nintendo's policies with other developers meant that the developers produced titles for their format exclusively for two years. While the effort of European developers flourished, in the US the Master System had only two third party developers, meaning the selection of games was flimsy at best.

The Master System was a console full of potential, but lacking in any real support. Classic games can be found on the format — the original *Phantasy Star*, with it's groundbreaking visuals, is still playable today alongside its online counterpart; *Alex Kidd* and *Wonder Boy*, two would-be Mario contenders, at the time offered great platforming experiences. The SMS takes its place in videogaming history as the first of many Sega systems that would unfortunately end up being overlooked by the public, and ruined by its closest rival's grip on the market.

For Nintendo, their trouncing of Sega was only one factor in many proving their success and proliferation of the market. In 1988, Nintendo sold another seven million NESs in the US. And while they were not going to fully rest on their laurels, they may have underestimated Sega…

The 16-Bit War (1989-94)

Platform wars. My computer vs. your computer. Petty squabbles, yes, but ones that were reflected in the manufacture and marketing of the machines in this period. Atari, Commodore, Sega, Nintendo – they all pitched in during some of the most active years in videogaming.

Atari vs. Commodore

The technologies for home computing were moving on. IBM PCs were slowly making their way into the home and along with the outstanding graphics on games in the arcades and home consoles; they were highlighting the limitations in the likes of the ZX Spectrum and C64. In 1982, a team of designers started work on a project to create a home console that would rival the powerful arcade machines of the time. The project evolved as years went on: an operating system was created to run the machine, previously unheard of in games programming, and this was a turn that would take the machine more towards being a home computer than a console. Female code names were used for the project, as a way of deflecting an interest from those eavesdropping on their conversations; the project was labelled 'Lorraine', which eventually morphed into Amiga, being Spanish for girlfriend.

In 1985, Commodore founder Jack Tramiel bought Atari's floundering computer division from Warner Communications, and left the company he had helped create. He left after disagreements over nepotism: he wanted his sons to work for Commodore, but other Commodore executives did not. Tramiel wanted revenge, and thought he could turn the failing company around to challenge Commodore. Atari had dabbled in the home market, but they were unable to keep with the steamrollering sales of the C64, and after 1984 few people were willing to give the Atari name a chance. Meanwhile, Commodore pressed on with newer systems, with claims that it would be the first 16-bit computer. When Tramiel heard of the Amiga project, which had now developed into a 16-bit home computer-cum-games machine, he decided that it would be the perfect computer to help reverse Atari's fortunes. Commodore wasn't going to just sit by and watch them snap up this well developed/ researched product, so they offered to buy the computer the Amiga Corporation were working on. Atari were enraged—they had even loaned the Amiga team money to ensure swift development—but Commodore and their bank balance won out, and the Amiga was theirs.

As the new Commodore-Amiga Inc. investigated viable ways of introducing their machine to the market, Atari fought back, quickly assembling their own 16-bit computer, the ST, which was quicker to build and produce, and eventually beat Commodore to the shopfloor. The ST sold quite well, having numerous advantages over the then current crop of home computers. By the time the first Amiga, the Amiga 1000, made it to stores Commodore couldn't instantly beat the lead Atari had, especially at a cost of over £1000. By 1986, Atari's accounts were finally in the black, with their net income for that year standing at £25million. But patience was going to pay off for Commodore. A few Amiga variants later, and the A500 was launched in 1987. It appeared at just the right moment for many who were finding their stalwart Spectrums and C64s were going out of date; and the increasing range of games made the Amiga quite a desirable computer. By Christmas 1989 special deals incorporating the Amiga and a pack of games were the gifts of choice for families; retailers offered similar bundles for the Atari ST also. In mid 1990, Commodore announced sales of 200,000 A500s

Both the Amiga and the ST had their individual strengths and weaknesses, but Amiga seemed to be winning the fight. They may not have set the whole world on fire—the real ST vs. Amiga phenomenon was limited to Europe, and while the two would eventually be overshadowed by the IBM PC's proliferation of the market and higher power, the period of time when home computers were all about the Atari vs. Commodore platform war is as important to many as the Speccy and C64 years were.

Some Handy Developments: Nintendo vs. No One

Nintendo held the home videogames market in the palm of their hand, and weren't willing to loosen their grip, deciding instead to focus on handheld gaming as a method of strengthening their presence in the market.

Handheld gaming was an area Nintendo was already partly familiar with. Back in 1980, when Nintendo had just started their American subsidiary, they launched the Game and Watch (G&W) series. These were small electronic games using liquid crystal display (LCD) for the graphics, designed by Nintendo staffer Gumpei Yokoi. They weren't groundbreaking or new at this point: LCD and electronic games had first appeared in the late 1970s, and successful derivatives, like the Simon game, etc., were very popular in the late 1970s/80s and have since become iconic items of childhood nostalgia for many. What was important about this branch of gaming was it's execution. Following their launch in 1980, G&W became a mini-brand, epitomising all that Nintendo was, and to some extent still is; (mostly) affordable, well made games, with distinctive hardware. G&W was the first kind of electronic entertainment to brandish a D-pad, a directional digital pad to control up, down, left, and right, always laid out on Nintendo hardware as a small + shape. The success of these devices would last into the decade, and they paved the way for Yokoi's future success, the Game Boy.

The Game Boy was different to the G&W range, though. Instead of being capable of playing just one game, the handheld device would, like the consoles before it, play games from cartridges. The difference being that the GB would display the games on a small B&W screen. The Game Boy unit was launched in 1989, featuring the now familiar d-pad and A-B buttons (like its cousin, the NES, and the G&W ancestors); it was affordable, lightweight and portable. It also came with the game *Tetris*, a wise move for Nintendo, as the brilliantly simple speed and puzzle game was to become iconic with players around the world.

But the Game Boy wasn't to be the only hand held launched in 1989. The year also saw Atari's attempts to claw back into the videogames market with the Lynx. The Atari Lynx was many things: powerful, it boasted a full colour screen, offered an enticing line-up of games, and even featured a cunning symmetrical design that allowed use by both right handed and left handed players. But it was rubbish when used in the real world. Heavier than a brick and hugely battery hungry: you'd be lucky to get four solid hours of play before you had to change AAs. A power supply lead was available, but it negated the point of having a portable device. Against the might of the Game Boy, the Lynx was near enough dead on arrival—an unfortunate turn that would plague Atari from this point on.

The Game Boy, despite the limitations highlighted by Atari's machine, was to become the dominant force in handheld gaming, and to an extent the only real viable platform for portable gaming. Between 1989-1992, the machine sold 6million units in Europe alone. As we will later learn, the device became a corner stone for Nintendo, a shield that they would rely upon to fend off other similar devices, and a lifeline when their other decisions led them down somewhat rockier paths.

Sega vs. Nintendo

After the Colecovision, the next 16-bit machine was NEC's PC Engine, which ran games from both small 'Hu-Cards', and also, revolutionary for the time, CDs. It wasn't a full 16-bit machine, despite what the NEC Press Office claimed; the processor was an 8-bit chip, but it did have a powerful graphics chip and the unit was capable of dealing with the large volumes of information stored on the Hu-Cards. Launched in 1988 in Japan, the machine soon grew in popularity, and by 1989 was outselling the Famicom for sales that year.

Sega was buoyed by their moderate success in Europe, and despite their low market share in the American and Japanese home videogame market, they decided to jump ahead of the competition with a device based on the System 16 motherboard that was allowing them to create such fantastic arcade games. The machine, the Mega Drive, debuted in 1989 in Japan and sold quite well. The launch line-up featured arcade conversions; like the tactics used earlier in the decade by American manufacturers, Sega were promoting the idea that the machine would allow gamers to play perfect replicas of coin-op games in their living rooms. At the time of Japanese launch, however, it was still not possible to strongly compete with either the Famicom's continued popularity or the PC Engine's userbase—the latter had gained a library of over a hundred games in 1989 alone. It was going to take a little effort for Sega to prove itself.

Two consoles launched in the US in 1990; the Neo-Geo and TurboGrafx-16 (which was the western name for the PC Engine). The Neo-Geo was a high quality machine, offering near-exact versions of arcade games but because of this the price point for the machine and the games remained high—while it offered exceptional quality games, sales never took off to match other competitors, and the console remains something solely for the hardcore gamer. NEC's console also failed to take off Stateside; it's games were not Americanised enough for the audience it was hoping to appeal to, whereas Sega's machine was ready to offer full 16-bit quality, and a better line up of games.

It was a slow fight for Sega, but they were winning. Their nearest techno-logical rivals were failing to set the scene alight, and it was time to show them how it was done. At this point, Sega's image was all about the 'new'; their new machine boasted powerful play, a sleek black design, and an ergonomic control pad. For the 1990 launch in the US, the console was renamed Genesis, promoting this idea of rebirth and newness to gamers. It worked, by Christmas 1990, the Sega Genesis was the most demanded console that year.

Better late than never, Nintendo entered the 16-bit arena with the Super Famicom (known in the US and Europe as the Super NES or Super Nintendo and hereon referred to as SNES). As it was developed a year after its main competitor, Sega's Mega Drive, it was billed as the most powerful machine around. An internal Sony-supplied sound clip certainly was ahead-of-the rest and the machine was also capable of creating some basic 3D effects, although some games required an extra 3D processing chip to be built into the cartridges, pushing up their price, but proving Nintendo were willing to go all-out to create great looking games. At launch, all SNES machines came with the game *Super Mario World*, featuring their stalwart mascot.

Sega refused to let Nintendo just arrive on the scene, and they fought back with a small nocturnal animal that moved at uncharacteristically high speeds. *Sonic The Hedgehog*, featured Sonic, Sega's new company mascot—he repre-sented the edgier image that Sega wanted to be associated with. Mario, an old man with his bright colours and slow jumping, was for juveniles. Sonic, who tore through huge levels at high speeds, was for grown-ups; he had a character and personality that made Sega cooler; he was a cynical antidote to jumping and collecting coins. Plus there was a cute ecological message behind his adventures: his games were essentially quests against the evil techno-lord Robotnik who enslaved fluffy wildlife animals for nefarious deeds. Via Sonic, Sega managed to steal the younger audience that Nintendo could usually fall back on, while appealing also to older gamers. Sega hit at the heart of Nin-tendo's fan base, and while some of their other titles lacked some of the qual-ity that marked the Nintendo product, they certainly matched their Japanese rival with all-round content.

The rivalry between Nintendo and Sega was huge, with each company aggressively trying to match the other company like-for-like. Gamers were caught in a tug of war between which brand they preferred, but the competi-tion between the companies at least allowed the gamer a wide variety of peripherals and games for whatever system they chose. When Nintendo announced the Super Scope light gun, Sega announced the Nemesis gun; while the SNES had Capcom's successful *Street Fighter 2*, the Mega Drive had *Streets of Rage* available.

Sega matching Nintendo's output (and vice versa) did not end with their rival 16-bit machines. 1991 saw the launch of the Game Gear, Sega's answer to the Game Boy. Cunningly built around the architecture of the Master System (it could even play SMS games via an add-on), the machine boasted a full colour screen and exclusive Sega titles. Unfortunately, like the Atari Lynx, it ate batteries for breakfast, plus software support from third party publishers was poor, incomparable to the expanding software range of titles available for Nintendo's handheld machine. Despite the availability of an add on that allowed the machine to be turned into a small television, the Game Gear did not offer a sufficient enough draw away from the Game Boy. Sega were winning the battle for space under the telly, but had lost the war in the portable market.

Sega had the larger share of the market and they wanted to keep things that way. In order to do this, their strategy was to keep the Mega Drive very current and up-to-the-minute with new technology. The result, however, was messy and poorly received. The first was the Mega CD (MCD). This was a unit that sat under the Mega Drive, and as the name suggests, played CD-based software. The unit enhanced sound, played music CDs, and allowed the playback of full motion video (the Japanese market even featured a Karaoke-add-on that played to these strengths). At the time of the unit's development in 1991, FMV was tipped to be the defining factor in the future success of video games, as this would allow the success of 'interactive movies' (a phrase that these days can induce as much fear in a gamer as 'edutainment'). A large proportion of developers attempted to make these interactive films/games, but they were all of poor quality. The Phillips PC-I and the Amiga CDTV had proven that this was an idea relatively dead on arrival. Limited gameplay and bad acting were just two of the thousands of complaints to level at the sub-genre. The real setback to Sega's unit was that along with its ridiculous price, it did nothing to improve the graphics of the Mega Drive. Why bother with a system that doesn't offer a visible improvement in quality, and barely improved the other specifications of the machine? Plus, development companies woefully under supported the system. With these inherent flaws, the Mega CD became something only for the hardcore Sega fan.

The 32X was Sega's next attempt to secure its fan base with 'impressive' technology, launched in 1994, and was marginally more successful. The unit plugged into the Mega Drive cartridge slot and increased the console's power using 32-bit processors. The unit had dedicated 32X games only compatible with that unit. In some ways, the device was another attempt to ensnare those who visited arcades back into the living room. Versions of *Virtua Fighter*, *Virtua Racing*, and the immensely popular *Star Wars Arcade* existed on the 32X and were all fairly adequate. A port of *Doom* also existed. Plus, the unit could work with the Sega CD, increasing the resolution of the games available. However, as with the CD unit, the 32X was plagued with price point problems, a lack of support from software developers, and apathy from gamers, so the add-on eventually floundered.

Sega's peripherals were desperate attempts to secure their place in the market, but their attempts backfired, and to some, it felt that their brand was crumbling, cheapened by their failure. Plus, the rumours were already rife that Sega had another 32-bit unit in production, so why bother with these stopgaps? With disappointing game backlists for these expensive uber-platforms, gamers had every right to be disappointed in Sega and their 'new' systems. Videogamers were ready for something really new, and despite Sega's attempts to harness the approaching 32-bit future for themselves, the 32-bit revolution was around the corner, and far greater that anyone would have expected...

Later Years: Forgotten Failures

The first of these was 1993s Atari Jaguar. Billed as the first 64-bit console, Atari were hoping that the machine would enable them to re-enter the market they had created. Yet this attempt was for nought. A confusing launch (the Jaguar was originally to be the successor to an Atari 32-bit machine) meant that the console launched to late after the Mega Drive and SNES had launched and established their user base, and too early to get caught in the wave of next generation fever that Sega and Sony's new rumoured machines offered. Development for the system was tough, too, and it took a while for decent games to emerge. Plus, the controller was possibly the worst ever designed for a system; uncomfortable, with a ridiculous numerical pad which, as well as being a throw back to the Atari peripherals of old, we can only assume looked good on paper. The machine only sold 200,000 units in its first year on the market, and while Atari kept promoting the device into the early stages of the PlayStation age (they even released a CD unit for the machine), it seemed to offer far too little in comparison to what was already available from other, cheaper systems.

Most interestingly in 1993, was the launch of The 3DO Company. This was a consortium of manufacturers and developers, including Electronic Arts, AT&T, and Matsushita, one of Japan's largest electrical manufacturers. The aim was simple: using their combined knowledge and financial force, they would devise a 32-bit CD-based home console. Other companies could license and manufacture their own machines, with The 3DO Company acting as a monitoring board for what essentially would be a unified format for videogaming. Panasonic and other electronics manufacturers produced 3DO machines, and the range of titles available was a strong enough start against what the already established consoles had. The real barrier, however, was the price; at $700, the machine never had a chance. Plus, the 3DO premise, while theoretically sound, would never be strong enough to compete with the variety on offer (and promised) by the other large forces that dominated the market

Even these large multinationals can make mistakes, however, and Nintendo made a big one in 1994, with their Virtual Boy. Virtual Reality was a bit of an outdated concept by now, having briefly been heralded as the future of gaming (the concept being players wear special headsets which make them feel they were in a real, three dimensional world), but eventually critics and cynics were put off my the chunky equipment and poor games. But Nintendo seemed oblivious to the criticism, and took a chance on the machine being devised by Game Boy creator Gumpei Yokoi which cashed in on the craze for VR technology. The result was a static headset, on a stand, which players had to position correctly on a table and lean into. Graphics were generated in red on two small screens inside the headpiece. Even with the Nintendo name behind it, the machine attracted barely any users, and after the poor launches in Japan and the US, Nintendo made the decision not to launch the console in Europe.

The PlayStation Age (1995-1999)

PC-ness Gone Mad

Until the early nineties the viability of the IBM PC as a games platform was understated. As time passed, smaller home computers found more ways of entering the home. Nowadays, when we refer to a 'PC' (personal computer), we are referring to a machine that has evolved from the IBM type, which first debuted in 1981. IBM PCs were originally designed solely for serious users; they were the mainstays of businesses, and those that were available to buy were not marketed for their games playing powers. The technology that an IBM PC is composed of is non-specific: each needs a processor, memory, etc, but these can vary in speed and type, and are made by various manufacturers. The interchangeable nature of this format is what gave rise to the proliferation of its use—businesses could chose the components they required at the price point they could afford, and upgrade and change parts as technology improved.

The PC was not overlooked as a games platform throughout the 1980s; it was more of a fringe platform. Developers of more 'high brow' gaming were the mainstays for the format. As the likes of the Commodore and Atari brands died off, many consumers gradually switched to PCs. But the fact that they were of an unspecified nature meant that the consistency between machines was lax. Software developers would not know what the 'average' system was, so designing games and programs was somewhat hit-and-miss: there was a chance that the hardware variations could not handle certain software.

IBM introduced the VGA standard for PC graphics in 1987, meaning that up to 256 colours could be displayed on screen, far better than the home consoles of the time, the NES and SMS. By 1990 CD-ROM soon became a viable format, and with it, multimedia (a fancy word for incorporating graphics, sound, video, text, to create new experiences). To make sure that computers were of a uniform standard the Multimedia PC Marketing Council proposed a baseline definition of what internal components were needed to perform/utilise multimedia on an IBM. To bring computers up to speed, various manufacturers released soundcards and CD-ROM drives, and games were being produced around these peripherals. Until this point, sound, if needed, was generated with speakers built into the machines—the speakers were really only capable of making beeping and grunting noises—now, however, with CDs and specialist sound units, PCs had became advanced audio visual devices.

The PCs user base continually grew with its constantly advancing graphical powers, but there was one thing that the platform currently did not offer: 3D graphics. The SNES and Jaguar had offered 3D to a limited extent, and Sony was boasting how it was the centrepiece of their PlayStation, but the technology had not yet made its way to the PC. By 1995, however, the chips needed to process the swathes of info to generate decent 3D polygons were affordable, and various manufacturers were producing cards capable of throwing high-resolution graphics around the screen. Also, because so many companies had a vested interest in brining 3D graphics to the PC, the competition was such that research and the technology available pushed things along faster. The PC's position as a viable gaming platform was finally consolidated, and the next few years would see the platform successfully compete with the PlayStation, N64 and the other consoles available until the present, where PC Gaming could almost be classed a sub division of gaming all of its own.

The Troubled Birth of the PlayStation

At the time of writing, the Sony PlayStation is the world's biggest selling home console. The events that led up to its launch, are however, some of the most interesting in games history. At one point it was going to be called the Nintendo Play Station...

Before the release of the SNES, Sony worked with Nintendo to design the SNES-CD drive. The SNES units were manufactured with an extension port in its underside in order to utilise such a device should it be released. The deal with Sony, however, worried Nintendo; the contract stated that if the machine went into production, the CDs would be solely manufactured by Sony. The SNES, with a CD drive, would really be a half-Nintendo, half-Sony machine. Plus, Nintendo felt that cartridges, with their faster loading times, were far more appealing to gamers than CDs. Nevertheless, the two companies continued their joint research.

Meanwhile Philips, a major Sony-rival, became the first manufacturer to release a CD-based entertainment machine, the CD-I. It attempted to be more of an all-rounder in home entertainment, playing educational games, and videogames, and a proprietary form of Video CD movies (as well as standard Video CDs, VCD being a very popular video medium in Japan and the rest of Asia). Like the MCD, there was an over reliance on full motion video, although this made porting some arcade games easier (*Mad Dog McCree*, for instance). In attempting to appeal to the family, they focused far too much on educational titles and family movies; their game titles were weak.

At the 1991 Consumer Electronics Show, Sony announced that their deal with Nintendo had produced the Play Station. The PS would play CD games as well as have a cart slot for SNES cartridges. The machine would also be able to play VideoCDs. However, Nintendo had other ideas at CES. The next day, they announced that they were now working with Philips to create a SNES-CD drive, breaking their contract with Sony. (Philips in turn had licence to use Nintendo characters on their CD-I; later in the short and useless life of the device, Nintendo characters Link, Mario, and Luigi would all appear on the format, albeit in overly kid-friendly games.) This took Nintendo into dangerous territory—Sony were furious that Nintendo dared to deal with their biggest rival (a non-Japanese one no less), they could have forced legal action, and the Japanese business world could turn on Nintendo now that it had displayed such backhanded tactics. Still, the two companies remained friendly; Sony still wanted to have a SNES cartridge slot on their machine, and Nintendo relied on Sony to supply the audio chips for the SNES. In 1992, it seemed the deal was back on, but in an altered form; the SNES-CD and

Sony PlayStation would be two independently manufactured units, but they would be compatible.

Sony units went into production and then quickly out of production. Why? Believing that cartridge-based games were reaching their life expectancy, Sony realised that a machine with a cartridge slot would be useless in the long-term. This and the other disagreements with Nintendo meant the deal was eventually dissolved. Officially, both companies claimed that they had only been working together for a month, when in truth their cooperation had been quite lengthy and productive: three versions of the Nintendo PlayStation existed: the CD add-on for the SNES, the standalone Nintendo brand CD console (a device that looked like a CD-ROM drive with a loading slot, utilising the SNES controller), and the chipset allowing others to license and manufacture their own machines.

Sony were left with their half of the deal; the CD technology, and stuck with it, incorporating new technology to improve chip design. A cheaper design was chosen (the loading slots proving quite expensive at the time) and Sony set about making a controller of their own. The real card up Sony's sleeve, however, was their 3D technology. Having researched its use for sometime, the processing ability of the PlayStation's graphics chips was, at the time, over whelming.

The PlayStation launched in 1995, facing off against a similar machine from Sega. Sega's machine was the long-rumoured Saturn, also a CD-based console. At launch, it cost $100 more than the Sony machine, and was pretty much second in the race that year, unable to compete with Sony thereafter. Sega had launched the machine earlier than originally stated, and to many it looked as if Sega were scared by the future promise of the PlayStation. Also, consumers had somewhat lost faith in Sega, their name tarnished by their cheap add-ons in previous years, and in Japan and Europe, the PlayStation was a more attractive proposition, with a stronger line up of games. In the Saturn's life span (up to 1998), it sold poorly, despite a growing user base in Japan. To an extent this was a disappointment for the Sega fans, as the machine, while expensive, did have some quality titles, just not enough to sustain interest from the mass market.

Nintendo too tried to forge on, announcing that they would be jumping straight to a 64-bit machine, at the time called 'Project Unreality', later known as 'Ultra 64', but finally called the Nintendo64 (N64). The unit's design was undertaken with Silicon Graphics, whose machines were responsible for the computer rendered art in movies, and other powerful supercomputers. Nintendo chose to go against the current grain and stick with cartridges instead of CDs; cartridges were better protection against games piracy, but were expensive to produce, unlike CDs. This was going to prove to be part of the machine's undoing.

The N64 launched in 1996, and the graphics for the likes of *Super Mario 64* were certainly impressive. The launch was at the time the most successful so far in games retail. But already, the N64 was behind the crowd, despite a technological advantage. The PlayStation was already significantly cheaper, and Nintendo's dropping the cost to an equal price point just looked like desperation. At the same time, the games available came out sporadically, and many were just remakes or reuses of Nintendo's NES and SNES licences. While many of the games' joy lay in their execution, it was the choppy and predictable line-up that gradually put gamers off. There were not enough games to beat Sony. Also, Nintendo were confusing some people; they were still releasing the odd game for the SNES and the awful Virtual Boy had cheapened their image. As time went on, the outlook for the N64 was bad, despite huge successes like *The Legend of Zelda: The Ocarina of Time*, which became the fastest selling game of all time. While championed by many gamers, Nintendo was not winning the home console race.

In Sony, the PlayStation had a parent company willing to wait. They had previous experience in all kinds of home entertainment electrics, and they had the money and time to spend building a user base. With a quality software line-up, enough games to satisfy each demographic, coupled with clever marketing twists (demo pods in popular night clubs, for instance), Sony managed to slowly push the PlayStation into the global gaming consciousness, directing attention first away from Sega, and then Nintendo. The PlayStation became the leading champ in videogaming, and its longevity and success is so far unrivalled by any other console. Sony's trouncing of Sega meant they also absorbed a good portion of their rival's installed base; to Sega fans who felt the Saturn's crash and burn, Sony was an escape plan. They were able to remain faithful to a cheaper, CD-based format, and still fly in the face of their other 'enemy' Nintendo.

Nintendo's Golden Boy

Nintendo was still winning one battle, however, and that was the portable gaming war. Sales of the Game Boy were consistently strong, even ten years after its debut. This was partly down to the fact that in the handheld arena they faced little to no competition. Both SNK and Bandai had tried to enter the Japanese market in 1999 (with the Neo-Geo Pocket and Wonderswan, respectively), but their efforts failed to catch the attention Nintendo had. No other company would be able to compete with the vast library of titles available for the Game Boy.

An improved version of the Game Boy, smaller, lighter, with a slightly better screen was released in 1996, keeping things ticking over for Nintendo. Luckily, resurgence was heading their way starting in Christmas 1998. Nintendo released the Game Boy Camera, a rudimentary device that allowed the GB to act as a digital camera. A printer was also released allowing these digital photos to be printed as stickers. The jewel in Nintendo's crown over these years year was, however, the Game Boy Colour. Nintendo remade several of the classic GB games with extra levels that could only be played using the colour screen. At the same time, rumours were circulating that Nintendo were fast at work on a successor to the Game Boy, a more powerful handheld device, 32-bits, making it twice as powerful as the SNES.

Nintendo's future in handheld gaming already seemed certain, but was about to get a major boost throughout 1999 and 2000, thanks to that little phenomenon, *Pokémon*. Launched in 1996 in Japan, the franchise made it's way to the US in 1998. It was an RPG in which your character had to travel the world and collect countless magical animals, called *Pokémon*. The hook lay in the fact that there were two versions of the game available, and you could only catch all the *Pokémon* if you linked the two versions together using two Game Boys; it didn't hurt that the game was addictive, well made, and exceedingly playable by anyone of any age. The fever was on, as kids across the globe clamoured for the game and a machine to play it on. The game was matched with a sizeable level of marketing, including the standard merchandising and a rather good cartoon; Nintendo were practically given a licence to print money as parents and gamers handed over cash to satisfy the craze of 'Gotta catch em all!' (the franchise's slogan). In an ironic twist, one of the spin-off products was a card game which gained more notoriety and popularity than its videogame inspiration, and Nintendo had returned full circle to producing the types of cards they were making over a hundred years previously.

It was *Pokémon* that saved Nintendo from the doldrums in the late 90s. Despite the increasingly quality line up of games for the N64, the Game Boy was their real success story, still drawing gamers in a decade after launch. At the same time, Nintendo, Sega, and Sony were all looking to the next generation, as rumours flew that they were all working on their own new machines that would revolutionise home gaming…

The Connected Age (1999 and beyond)

The Internet has gone from being a mysterious new media to a multi-faceted tool, relied upon by all walks of life. Connection is now the driving force in technology, and this has been reflected in the growing use of mobile phones and the rise of the Internet. Videogaming has been interwoven with the expansion of online technologies. In the same way that games spun out of early computer research, games eventually made their way into the research of early computer networks. As it soon became clear that computers across the world could share information, this fact was exploited to allow people in different locations to play against each other.

A History of Online Gaming

Online gaming (and multi-player online gaming) really started in the early sixties with the creation of PLATO, the computer network founded at The University of Illinois, which spread to other college campuses as it grew in popularity. In hindsight, several years later, an acronym was created for the name: Programmed Logic for Automatic Teaching Operations. While it would be a teaching device, it was also used for fun: in 1969 a 2-player version of *Spacewar!* was created for PLATO, with users playing against others based at terminals on the other side of the campus. As well as games, PLATO also allowed users to chat to each other, incorporated a bulletin board system similar to ones on the net today and included email too. By 1972 PLATO could support 1000 users at the same time. More advanced games, such as *Empire*, which could support up to 32 players, came later on (approx. 1974). In *Empire*, inspired by *Star Trek*, you could play as one of four teams: Federation, Romulan, Klingon or Orion with an aim to take over every planet in the universe.

In 1978 work on the first MUD (Multi-User Dungeon) began at Essex University in the UK. The MUD offered a world various players could logon to and explore using typed commands (the game is otherwise best described as 'text based virtual reality'). In approximately 1980 MUD1 was completed and put online. It was fairly successful and was soon being passed around the world. In the early 80s companies started charging for access to online games via commercial networks. In 1984 the first commercial version of MUD1 became available on Compunet. Prices for access to these games usually started at around $5 an hour, but could go much higher, although games that only required a flat rate fee were also devised.

Towards the end of 1985 Quantum Computer Services launched a graphics based online service for Commodore 64/128 users known as QuantumLink. In the next year QuantumLink and Lucasfilm started work on another graphics based game, *Habitat*, that was very influential on some of the online games available today thanks to the game's use of graphical avatars and speech bubbles. Also in 1986 the first play by email game emerged for commercial networks, the *Rim Worlds War*, written by Jessica Mulligan. By the early nineties Quantum Computing had renamed itself America OnLine, but bigger changes were still to come. Up until now consumers had been using modems to access the online services of specific companies. Then DARPA-Net, a network used primarily by universities and government agencies, became known as the Internet, and various companies become Internet Service Providers.

At the very end of 1993 the revolutionary *Doom* was released. The classic first person shooter was extremely popular amongst players who would use LAN connections so that up to four gamers could play at once. When the web browser Netscape was released in 1994 it became much easier to access the web, and from this more opportunities to play games were discovered. Hundreds of MUDs became available on the net and many of them free of charge, drawing in both experts and newcomers, helping lay the foundations for the burgeoning online community.

In 1996 *Quake*, the follow-up to *Doom*, was released, and thanks to its online functions tens of thousands of players were soon logging on to kill each other on a daily basis. Online gaming really started to take off at this point and many more games were released with online components. In 1997 *Ultima* Online was released. *Ultima* quickly acquired thousands of players, in part because it was already a big name with several successful role-playing-game instalments behind it. Other popular massively multiplayer games that were released in the years after *Ultima* Online include Sony's *EverQuest* and Microsoft's *Asheron's Call*.

The New Generation

In the previous chapters, the Internet had yet to influence the console market, but that soon changed. The PlayStation is still arguably the dominant force in home videogaming, but these days Sega, Nintendo, Sony and even Microsoft have all tried to up the ante in home entertainment, with varying success.

Until 1998 online gaming had been the domain of gamers with personal computers. With the launch of Sega's Dreamcast this began to change. The Dreamcast was Sega's attempt to not only recapture a share of the market, but also to ride the wave of Internet hype. The machine was 128-bit, utilising a proprietary new type of CD-ROM; it also had an onboard modem for Internet access, and sumptuous graphics. The launch in 1999 was very successful, with the new machine selling well, beating other companies to the 128-bit punch.

Yet continued success was not on the cards for Sega. Their reputation as a hardware manufacturer was still slightly tarnished, while the Internet access forced use of Sega's proprietary ISP. Plus, marketing hyperbole from themselves and their rivals was to be their downfall. '6 billion players online' boasted advertisements over-ambitiously, but this was a misnomer especially when the online functions featured in many launch titles were quite limited. At the same time, the release of the Dreamcast was cunningly countered by Sony, with continued reports regarding their upcoming 128-bit machine, the PlayStation 2.

The PS2 launched in 2000. Graphically it was on par with what the Dreamcast, and was backward compatible with almost all the previous PlayStation (renamed the PSone) software. Most importantly it could play DVDs, and this became the unique selling point for the machine: it played games but was a rival to DVD players as well. For many people, the movie-playing capability was reason alone to buy a machine, upgrading from the original PlayStation, and the launch was a great success. The machine did not come with a modem however, and Sony made many statements that looked to the long-term, with claims that future modem and hard drive peripherals would help turn the PlayStation into the ultimate home entertainment system, as movies and games would be available for download. The idea is still being bandied about to this day, with only few details of how prepared Sony are paving the way for these entertainment 'hubs'.

In the short-term, however, the PS2 was overpriced, overhyped, and understocked. A supply problem meant that there were not enough units to meet demand, despite the attempts of a Sony-implemented preorder system through UK retailers. The launch games were nothing special and the device's DVD playback was buggy. Yet the device still sold 70,000 units in the UK, with all initially available units sold. Sony's bubble hadn't popped, but had deflated slightly. It was going to be a while for quality games to show up.

2000 had been a rocky year for Sega, with their efforts overshadowed by Sony's continued dominance and rumours of what Nintendo and Microsoft were planning to introduce to the market. Quality-wise, the Sega machine was the best choice for gamers, with countless brilliant original games released along with updates of many Sega franchises (*Sonic* and *Virtua Fighter*, for a start), but many failed to notice this until it was too late. In the beginning of 2001, Sega announced that it was to quit the hardware business, abandoning the Dreamcast, and change its focus to developing their distinctive software as third-party titles for other formats. In a development that would have once been inconceivable, Sega later announced that they would be developing *Sonic The Hedgehog* games for Nintendo's latest generation of hardware.

Nintendo's first effort during the 21st century has been to continue unchallenged in the handheld market and their successor to the Game Boy, the Game Boy Advance, launched mid-2001. The machine is more powerful than a SNES, with a colour screen, and a new horizontal design. Like the PS2, the new machine plays all the software available for its predecessor, but unlike the PS2 the launch and first wave of titles do not disappoint. There are some limitations (the screen is too dark, and the unit maybe too small for western hands) but the continued stream of high quality software does impress, and the ability to link four machines together and play from only one copy of a game is a great bonus.

Nintendo's real hopes, however, are riding on their GameCube. Launched a few months after the GBA, the console sees Nintendo's home gaming efforts finally move away from cartridges to cheaper CDs, using a proprietary mini-CD as the format of choice. Like the PS2 the machine does not come with a modem: that will come later for those users interested in playing online games, as Nintendo are wary of making the online experience the be-all-and-end-all of their console. But connectivity is coming into play in some forms, as the GBA can be connected to the GameCube. While this facet has yet to be fully exploited, the idea is intriguing, as franchises like *Sonic* and *Zelda* can conceivably feature a lot of cross over between handheld and home console versions—characters and information could be transferred from machine to machine. Also, the GBA itself can be used as a controller, offering players an extra screen to consult during play.

Finally, in the new wave of machines is the new kid on the block; the Xbox. Much speculation and rumour surrounded the machine right up to its launch in last 2001; cynics have been quick to brand it as just a stable PC. While the technology it is composed of is similar to that found in home computers, Microsoft's aim is clearly for the videogaming market, and not a PC gaming subculture. The Xbox is a mix of things that made the Dreamcast and PS2 unique—high-powered games, Internet connectivity and DVD playback. The machine comes Internet ready, and while the dedicated network to support this has only just been announced, the machine can also be connected to other Xboxes, a facet most capably demonstrated by the machine's acclaimed launch title, *Halo*.

Both Nintendo and Microsoft have entered (or re-entered) the market at a time where the PlayStation is still dominant in the homes of many gamers. It is still too early to judge how successful each of the big three will be in their various pursuits of connectivity. While offline games are still a huge priority to many, we will have to wait and see how connected home videogames really become. These are interesting times: three consoles now demand our attention, and videogaming is unquestionably here to stay.

The Future?

At the moment, it's not uncommon to be sat opposite someone on the Tube who is fiddling with a GBA. Even less surprising is to watch another commuter play a little game on their mobile phone. You can expect to see an increase in mobile gaming; the SMS boom two years ago was likely just the start of something bigger. We can expect games that go beyond licenced versions of Snake and Tetris, but these will not just be self-contained one-player affairs. The theory behind the Mobile Internet offers a lot of possibility, but WAP came and went, painfully slow loading times with it. It's not the end for mobile gaming, though: faster, more accessible features thanks to new methods like GPRS, which features an 'always on' connection. This technology moves us towards some level of hyper-connectivity, where everything and everyone are available to play with or against at the touch of a button.

'Online is the future of gaming', according to some. Sony and Microsoft are telling us how their machines can be all-in-one, super duper home entertainment hubs, thanks to their technology and broadband Internet. Not just games, but movies and music will be available via the Internet. Yet the Internet has been around for a while now, it is already here, and Nintendo for one don't want to gamble their entire future on online gaming.

What could we expect beyond the next ten years?

Some gamers idealistically hope that at some point things will dramatically change; that instead of rival hardware firms and varying games platforms that there will be one consistent single platform for console videogames, like DVD or CD. It is an optimistic thought, but one that is unlikely to come to fruition. Look how far the idea got 3DO in 1993. Not very. While it would be 'nice' to see a videogaming world that put the somewhat petty platform wars to one side, this very competition is what has kept videogames alive. A single format could lead to complacency and laziness. Where would the identity of the console be? After all, the past hardware generations have survived alone on being able to offer specific kinds of gaming experiences. 'Imagine a world where Nintendo and Sony and Microsoft were all helping each other out,' say the idealists, 'just putting aside differences to create the best games possible.' But they would have to agree to develop for this uniform machine, and all be ready to give up their pursuit of securing large market shares, something that has so far been the furthest thing from their minds. To compete is the nature of business; it's also the nature of games themselves and, to a wider extent, it is the nature of human nature.

Another interesting possibility is the idea of the 'celebrity' in gaming; in an age currently obsessed with movie star diets, this is the sort of angle on things we could expect. Perhaps games will come to equal sports? Steven Poole and Jonathan Margolis have mused upon this possibility, and championships for certain games have been conducted for a while now. Certain game players could become household names, famous for their efforts at whatever the current of the minute online first person shooter is. The designers of the games could be elevated to the level of rock stars… Or maybe not. The game playing experience is one that eschews the personality of the creators, and the only real person who is standing centre-stage is the player. It is the very nature of videogames to require participation, placing the player solely in control. Will we really prefer to watch someone ace the later levels of *GoldenEye*, rather than play it ourselves?

Luckily the future of videogames is not in question. The most important thing to remember is that they are here, and most likely here to stay. People have always wanted to play. By all accounts, they will keep playing.

The Games

The following section lists 129 specifically selected games, sorted historically and by genre. It would impossible to list all the games for each genre, so instead what we present here are highlights of the past thirty years. Some are personal favourites, some are classics, some are revolutionary, and others are games that, while not of the greatest quality, are important artefacts of the media and the specific genre. This is not a definitive list, and you may disagree with some of our reviews. What this should do is paint a picture of the vast videogaming world, with its many styles and varying types of gameplay, all of which are, predominantly, fun and enjoyable.

(The dates apply to the game's original release, regardless of territory. When the game has appeared on more than one machine we have chosen either the platform that it first appeared on, or whichever platform hosts the best version of the game.)

Arcade Ancestors

The individual game genres only really developed after the first spate of highly original games, varying in content, hence our opening Arcade Ancestors, which are linked solely by their coin-op origins. That early graphical flair helped pave the way for a media that still strives to surprise and impress. With large flashy cabinets and instantaneous pick-up-and-play controls, these games are some of the best from the peak of the arcade boom. While no specific genre links them, we can see the beginnings of shoot 'em ups, platformers, and action games, with all of the following relying on quick thinking, good judgement and dexterity. Most of all, however, they are simply entertaining, with ideas exploited to their fullest potential.

Asteroids (1979)

With minimalist black and white vector graphics, the aim is to scoot around a 2D plane in a small spacecraft blasting asteroids into pieces. What makes *Asteroids* special is its chaotic bent; the asteroids would split into smaller pieces, and spin off in opposite directions. You had to make good use of the crafts turning and thrusting controls in order to dodge the rocks flying at you.

Space Invaders (1979)

There is a horde of alien craft bearing down upon you; you have one weapon at your disposal and limited places to hide; destroy them or be destroyed. It is an iconic game now, and at the time was revolutionary, introducing gamers to a relentless round of button mashing and quick reflexes, much mimicked since. Invaders became so popular in Japan that it almost caused a coin shortage and the entire franchise has so far generated over £300 million worldwide.

Battlezone (1980)

A precursor to first person shooters, placing you in control of a tank, your mission being to eliminate other aggressive vehicles. Two joysticks were used for movement, and orders flashed up on screen explaining where the nearest foe was. The game was quite limited, but the unique cabinet, with a periscope view-slot confining your vision to a vector screen, helped create an atmosphere in an otherwise cold experience.

Pac-Man (1980)

Simple yet with amazing appeal. Move Pac-Man around a maze, eating small dots that are littered throughout the paths. At the same time you have to avoid the ghosts that are intent on hounding Pac-Man to an early grave. Vivid and memorable, the game relied on sharp wits and cunning dexterity. Plus, the four ghosts all behaved differently adding a great twist to the proceedings; energy dots would make the spectral fiends vulnerable, but only for a limited time, so you had to be quick when chasing them down.

Star Wars (1983)

Another vector graphics game, this time placing you in the pilot seat of Luke Skywalker's X-Wing, with a sequence of missions set during the Rebellion's assault on the Death Star. The game to a great extent relied on two extras to invoke thrilling play; the gravitas of the *Star Wars* licence and its associated sights and sounds, and also the great controller – a two-handed 'yoke' control stick – that made you feel as if you were part of the film.

Donkey Kong (1981)

Created by Shigeru Miyamoto as a way to rid Nintendo of surplus machines, *Donkey Kong* told the tale of a carpenter (initially called 'Jumpman', but renamed to Mario after Mario Segali, the landlord of the NOA office) who had to rescue his girlfriend from the clutches of an evil gorilla located at the top of the screen. The gorilla (the titular Kong) would throw all barrels at Mario, who the player had to navigate up parallel platforms in order to rescue his woman. One of the first platformers, the popularity of which was helped by the excellent graphics and great gameplay: jumps had to be timed correctly, and player judgement came into play when choosing to avoid or dodge oncoming obstacles.

Zaxxon (1982)

What made *Zaxxon* so alluring in 1982 was the colourful isometric 3D graphics, placing you at an entirely new perspective for shoot 'em up games. The craft you controlled now had an extra direction to contend with (up and down) so it was up to the player to work out what the correct height was for working your way through a huge fortress, while also fighting against the armed forces. The viewpoint could cause problems, as it was sometimes difficult to correctly judge the height of some obstacles until they were right in front of you.

Dragons Lair (1983)

When you sidled up to the machine the first thing that hit you were the graphics. Using laserdisc technology, Disney-eqsue animation graced the screen. Gameplay however, was scant: allegedly you control the movements of dragon hunter Dirk the Daring, when the truth wasn't as involving. An animated clip played, and you had to make the a choice using the joystick or buttons as to where Dirk would go or what he would do, then another clip played, and so on. The graphics alone were no excuse for such limited interactivity, which required no skill at all, just a good memory of what happens in what clips.

Mario Bros. (1983)

Donkey Kong's star hero Mario and brother Luigi are given their own game. The aim involves more jumping, this time through sewers, defeating an infestation of beasties and monsters. The game had similar gameplay mechanics to *Donkey Kong*, but with many touches (knocking platforms from below to tip enemies off, or jumping on monsters in order to defeat them) which would not only shape the future of the Mario games, but also countless other platform games.

Platformers

Jump! That's the key to platform games, as the player is required to use their dexterity, judgement and timing to get bouncing characters from one end of a level to the next. Predominantly viewed from a side-on 2D view, and typically using bright graphics. Some games rely on pixel perfect jumping whereas others have easier controls, where only a general familiarity with the controls is needed. Not as popular as it once was—many titles that once would have made perfect platform material are now 3D action adventures—but one of the original and the best of the genres.

Pitfall (1980: Atari VCS)

The jungle adventure platformer that was the first of the genre to cover multiple screens. At the time, the graphics were revolutionary, and the pitfalls themselves Were exhilarating to cross, requiring good timing and attention to the other objects moving around on screen. An option to travel through a tunnel network underneath the jungle meant you had to work out when it was best to stay below ground or face the terrors and resurface.

Manic Miner (1983: Spectrum) and Jet Set Willy (1984: C64)

Starring Miner Willy, these two platform games required you to lead the digger-by-nature chap through individual screens that had to be traversed using perfect timing. The original saw you exploring caves and collecting keys; the sequel required you to tidy up Willy's mansion after a rather rowdy party. Notoriously difficult, requiring some instances of successive pixel perfect jumping (the more inept player can wildly claim that the games are not possible to complete), but what the game managed to do on such limited hardware is an impressive achievement, and both games remain brilliantly taxing and playable.

Dizzy series (1988-91: C64)

There are several games in the series but most share the premise of a girlfriend or relation needing rescuing, where you must lead our egg shaped hero, the titular Dizzy, to their aid. Gameplay is a more forgiving version of *Manic Miner*, with an occasional dash of object retrieval in order to progress. A lack of a save feature and only a handful of lives made the games frustrating at times, but the variety and the oddly charming character made it a perennial favourite.

Sonic the Hedgehog (1990: Sega Mega Drive)

Mario's cooler, sleeker playground enemy wasn't just a hollow mascot; his debut game was an instant classic. The game cleverly mixed platform jumping with terrific speeds juxtaposed against the odd moment where speed wasn't an option. Sonic sometimes had to wait for some platforms to slide into view, impatiently tapping his foot as he did. The levels, simple in their accessibility, but with even enough multiple paths to tear through or explore, are a joy to replay, even a decade later.

Rainbow Islands (1990: Amiga)

A cutesy vertical scrolling platformer, the twist being that your character can muster up rainbows to act as temporary platforms, and which also help capture and destroy oncoming enemies (small bugs and angry looking sprites). Hardly revolutionary, but visually quite distinctive, featuring a steadily increasing difficulty level, items to collect, and power-ups that increase your rainbow power.

Prince of Persia (1991: Amiga)

Motion captured *Arabian Nights*-style animation made this platformer a joy to behold on its debut, and it still stands some of the tests of time today. The plot is typical escape-from-the-dungeon-and-rescue-the-princess stuff, it is the levels that make the game so great: avoid pitfalls traps and death from falling great heights, and make it through closing gates just on time. A slight over reliance on pixel perfect jumps and specifically timed controls may seem frustrating to some, but the trial-and-error is half the fun—you only have an hour to rescue the princess, which helps create mounting tension and atmosphere to die for.

Super Mario World (1991: SNES)

While it bears heavy similarities to its predecessors, albeit with a cleaner, brighter design, the real stand out element is the depth and variety, and what is over all an outstandingly smooth experience. The length and scope of the game (spanning, as the title suggests, the whole Mario World) is not only impressive, but also a joy to behold, and is lovingly animated. Hidden bonuses and areas allow you to revisit the superb vistas. Our one complaint would be the button layout; on either SNES or GBA version, optimum control of our favourite plumber requires him to be continually running, but maintaining this leaves the player with hook fingers clawed around the buttons.

Super Star Wars series (1992-95: SNES)

Jump about the *Star Wars* universe in this fantastic series of games (there was one for each of the original trilogy), taking the guise of various characters. The games take complete liberty with the plots to the films, but that is beside the point: the scope of each level, and the quantity, makes this fun to return to. Extra spice is supplied by the use of Force powers in the later games, and the occasional ability to control vehicles.

Super Metroid (1994: SNES)

There is something brilliantly cinematic about the SNES's venture into the world of Samus Arran. Following on from the original NES *Metroid*, the Mother Brain must again be defeated and it is up to Samus to adventure and explore. A platform game with RPG leanings (perhaps comparable to *Baldurs Gate: Dark Alliance* in its association with the RPG genre) it is remarkable not only for great gameplay, but also from its stunning atmosphere. The design ethic smacks of quality and high tech beauty.

Mario 64 (1996: N64)

Mario makes the transition to three dimensions, and along the way manages to reinvent himself and his world. Yet again, Princess Peach has been kidnapped, and it is up to Mario to come to the rescue – her vast castle offers avenues to countless enjoyable and varying territories to search and conquer. Unlike the linearity of *Super Mario World*, *SM64* leans heavily towards exploration, with all areas requiring repeated attempts to have completely seen everything. Despite the odd camera problem (possibly acceptable given this was one of Nintendo's first forays beyond 2D) new controls and jump mechanisms add a breath of fresh air to platforming, Mario can now triple jump to hard to reach areas and even rebound up walls to high levels.

Action Adventure

This genre has morphed from platformers and supplanted them as the generic genre of choice given the increase in 3D processing power. The emphasis is often on third person perspectives, and sometimes the location of the camera becomes an important part of the action, with either fixed views, cameras that follow the characters, or cameras controlled by the player. Dexterity and coordination are relied upon for weapons use and puzzle solving. Based on exploration as well as linear movement between locations or across areas, these third person games tend to offer more immediacy, and are more pick up and play.

Adventure (1979: VCS)

Simple graphics utilised for greatness. The aim is simple: find keys and navigate the twisty paths outside a castle all the while trying to avoid all bats and dragons. Your task was to move your avatar around dodging enemies and navigating mazes. Said avatar may only have been a chunky pixel, but the game shines (and still remains playable today) by virtue of its puzzle solving and object manipulation elements. Low-tech class.

It Came From the Desert (1989: Amiga)

What makes this game so special is its pulp sci-fi plot—featuring giant killer ants—and its continually varied gameplay. Controlling a professor in a small US town, you are given the task of investigating a strange meteor crash. What ensues is some magically crafted stuff, part adventure game, part action, with some very basic first person shooting sections. Stylistically it is flawless, and despite the fact that it came on multiple disks (resulting in some laborious load times), it remains a testament to the quality of software that was available for the Amiga.

Alone In The Dark (1992: PC)

A creepy gothic ghost story, where you take the role of one of two people investigating some strange goings on. The first game to experiment with differing camera angles and how they effect the player's interaction with areas in a 3D screen, it eventually spawned sequels of its own and has a heavy stylistic influence on the *Resident Evil* series. While the experience doesn't last very long, it certainly is captivating and chilling, but the blend of action, adventure, and puzzle solving should keep you interested for the afternoon.

Tomb Raider (1996: PlayStation)

Yes, Lara Croft has got inhumanly large breasts, but the original *Tomb Raider* game was, and to many extents still is, a masterpiece. Many different ways existed to move Miss Croft, and generating her relic-hoping acrobatics were half of the fun; the huge areas to explore and puzzles to solve were the other half. Later adventures felt like carbon copies, and even worse soulless cashcows. The new PS2 version may be a return to form or a brave step in a new direction, provided Lady Lara hasn't been too inspired by Solid Snake.

Resident Evil (1996: PlayStation)

With touches influenced by *Alone in the Dark*, *Resident Evil* is a master-stroke in chilling gameplay. The plot revolves around the investigation of a zombie infestation, and offers a mixture of puzzle solving and weapon play. Where the game excels is in atmosphere—visually and audibly, playing the game can literally put you on edge, using all the devices (and then some) that horror film directors have relied on over the years to make you jump. Later iterations and spin-offs may have descended into schlock rubbish sequels, but that dirge still hasn't tarnished the brilliance of the original.

Metal Gear Solid (1998: PlayStation)

Hideo Kojima's groundbreaking game bridges a gap between gameplay and film; the cutscenes become cinematic hooks, replete with some top-notch voice acting (for videogames, at least). Stylistic touches exist that would make James Bond blush. And as for the game—stealth based espionage featuring all manner of possibilities—it is near perfect. The overly polished sequel moves towards fantastic levels of realism with its graphics, coupled with the same gameplay, but the glut of cutscenes in the successor only highlight what a per-fectly balanced game the first PlayStation iteration was.

Grand Theft Auto 3 (2001: PlayStation 2)

Steal cars, perform tasks for crime lords, dodge arrest. But here given a 3D execution to be jealous of. The opportunity for free roam is the real bonus—if you're tired of running errands for the latest mob boss, why not beat up some civilians for petty cash? Or steal fancy cars for performing crazy stunts in? The huge city you are given to explore is amazing in it's scope and detail, and breadth of extra things to do. An instant classic.

Baldurs Gate: Dark Alliance (2001: PlayStation 2)

Dungeons and Dragons without the pain. A fairly simple plot leads you, as a single character, through dungeon upon dungeon in order to stop evil unleashing itself upon the world. Remarkably different to its PC predecessors, the controls are simple and the stats are never rear their ugly heads for too long. The graphics are sumptuous; the only flaw is that the gameplay does get a little repetitive and tedious. The experience doesn't last particularly long, but a two-player co-operative mode extends the fun.

Ico (2001: PlayStation 2)

Short, sweet, and extremely pretty. Escape from a beautifully rendered castle, guiding a young girl with you. The joy arises from what isn't said in *Ico*; the music is minimalist, there are no ridiculously overblown cutscenes, the puzzles are demanding but cognitively fulfilling. Combat may be too simplistic, making for some tricky moments, but ninety nine percent of the time the game is perfection personified.

Adventure

The word 'adventure' is itself very broad. In using it here we are referring to those games that are a blend of puzzle solving and story: control of characters does not usually extend to combat and dexterity. Narrative is pushed to the fore and can only be developed via solving puzzles; the puzzles themselves require thought and experimentation rather than 'twitch' gaming. It was subject to a complete overhaul as graphics techniques improved (from completely text based to completely graphical), and have since almost died out as gamers favour more complex RPGs and action-heavy third person adventures. It is sometimes considered to be middlebrow entertainment: smarter than an arcade shooter, for sure, but not quite as demanding as, say, a statistic heavy strategy which requires a continued management of numbers and items. The lazy 'Sunday afternoon aspect' of these games is what we love—the games take a leisurely pace with often superbly surreal twists. It is just a shame that the genre with the most potential for variety ends up being the one with a slightly samey role call.

Adventure (1975: Apple II)

One of the early text based adventures that explored the ideas of 'interactive fiction'; passages of text explained a situation to a player, who had to type in commands (such as 'Go North') to navigate through the described milieu.

Most remarkable of the game's inception was that it truly was interactive in its creation; Will Crowther invented it, but the game was finished by another programmer, Don Woods, who added new rooms and perfected gameplay. The genre was much replicated with many different clones, the *Zork* series, and *The Hitchhiker's Guide to the Galaxy* (based on the book) being continual favourites throughout the 1980s.

King's Quest series (1985-1994: PC)

Sierra Games' adventure series was revolutionary, being the first game to offer adventure gamers scenes where a character could be moved around objects and interact with them. While the method of interaction was still via text input, and the actual game play seemed nothing other than moving from location A to location B, extra touches, like the surreal fairy tale humour in the second game, made the series fun to invest the occasional afternoon in.

Maniac Mansion (1987: Amiga)

The George Lucas-owned LucasFilm Games stepped into the adventure field, revolutionising control with a 'point and click' interface: use the mouse to select one of command from a list, and then point at objects and characters on screen to perform tasks. This and the Lucas adventures following had pulpy and enjoyable plots; *Mansion* spoofed 80s teen movies and trashy horror flicks, and its team of interchangeable characters added a brilliantly complex system of cooperative puzzle solving.

Zak McKracken (1988: Amiga)

Another LucasArts game, identical to *Mansion* in control, gameplay, and graphics. But the remarkable and memorable factor of *McKracken* was it's surreal plot (placing you in the role of the titular journalist investigating a three-headed squirrel and aliens from Mars, amongst other things) and abstract puzzles; up until then you would never have thought 'use stale bread on bus window' would glean any progress in a point 'n' click.

The Secret Of Monkey Island (1990: Amiga)

A cunning mix of ar-har matey atmosphere and Jolly Roger humour, which puts you in the shoes of wannabe pirate Guybrush Threepwood. More abstract puzzles from LucasArts, but most famously (and brilliantly) combat was included via banter swordplay—challenge someone to a fight and defeat them with the correct series of quips and cusses. *Island* was also responsible for the creation of a new dynamic music system for the Lucas games.

Sam And Max Hit The Road (1994: PC)

The first LucasArts game to do away with the list of commands. Instead, a series of icons could be switched between using the right mouse button. The command system was handled with aplomb, and suited the comic characters and design well. A modern classic that is still available on budget release with *Maniac Mansion* sequel *Day of the Tentacle*.

Grim Fandango (1998: PC)

One of the best point and click adventures available. A slightly dead skeleton known as Manuel Calavera spends his time sending the dead on their way, but then gets caught up in a conspiracy, which only he can solve. As to be expected from LucasArts, it's darkly funny, the graphics are glorious, and the control system fairly accessible, and there are no menus to wade through at all. A joy.

Broken Sword (2002: Game Boy Advance)

Cocky American tourist George Stobbart gets caught in a Parisian bomb blast, and his investigation of the event takes him on an Indiana Jones-esque adventure across the globe. This handheld conversion of an older PC/PlayStation point 'n' click fares exceedingly well thanks to a new and rather intuitive control system, which is a slight cross between that used by *Grim Fandango* and *Sam and Max*. Fairly well balanced—at times the action relies on too much talking—the entertaining puzzles and quirky humour suit the game's new portable home.

Role Playing Games (RPGs)

To an extent the 'role' is a misnomer; many of the following games are reliant on statistics to represent the growth of character strength, taking pointers from the Dungeons and Dragons games that somewhat inspired them. The real strength of RPGs lies in the consistent ability to provide epic stories set in huge worlds and offering you the chance to explore those kingdoms. They also tend to rely on turn based arena battles that rely on your ability to think out strategies and the use of commands rather than dexterity. Of recent times They have ousted adventure games as the choice for the more cerebral games player who wants story rather than strategy, but many lack the puzzle solving elements of their almost-deceased rival. Instead the focus is on power and combat and saving the world from destruction on a weekly basis.

Ultima series (1986-Present: PC)

The long established series of *Ultima* role-playing games contains many fantastical gaming gems. The online version (released 1997) is more of the same, but with a huge world that, like *EverQuest*, you feel you could get lost in. Graphics and gameplay are both simple but reliable, and as with most online games, it can be frustrating being a new player surrounded by those who are full of experience, but it is worth persevering—there is a lot of fun to be found.

Phantasy Star (1987: Sega Master System)

The first RPG to hit US shores, it was the success of this title that arguably ensured the future releases of other RPGs in the territory. The 3D/isometric perspectives were revolutionary at the time, and the thrilling story placed you at the centre of a galactic crisis that could lead to mass destruction. Linearity is kept low, and the mix of locations, puzzles and vehicles makes it a great challenge; far harder than the modern ilk of RPG, which can often be over-linear and restrictive.

The Legend Of Zelda: A Link To The Past (1992: SNES)

The SNES iteration of the *Zelda* saga is possibly the definitive game from the series, pre-N64 version. It offers all the amazing elements that make Link's various quests so much fun; various weapons and enemies are scattered across an epic quest spanning multiple universes. Not to be missed. Addicts can get an extra fix from the near-identical Game Boy variants (*Links Awakening*, and *Oracle of Ages/Seasons*) that are luckily a touch more taxing.

Secret of Mana (1993: SNES)

In the style of *Zelda*, one of the famous elements to *Mana* was that up to three-players could play cooperatively. Outstanding given that the RPG genre is notoriously single player. The graphics and music shine with craftsmanship—the latter especially—and a wide selection of weapons and sells mean that you can customise many elements to suit your own style of play.

Pokémon (1996: Game Boy)

An RPG that isn't just for children. You may despise the craze that has taken over the world, but give it a play and you'll probably change your mind. You play as a Pokémon collector who travels through the world to capture the little beasties known as Pokémon, and then battle them against others. There's lots of people to talk to and plenty of sub-quests too. However, if you intend to train up Pokémon to a particularly high level, you may find that the game gets a little boring.

Final Fantasy VII (1997: PlayStation)

A classic Japanese RPG with gorgeous graphics, an epic plot and gloriously angsty characters. *FF7* stands out amongst its counterparts in the series, but random battles irritate and gameplay is very linear at the beginning of the game. Overall, it's a great game with 70+ hours of fun. (Most instalments of the series are also worth purchasing, especially the Gameboy and SNES variants, although later games in the sequence have felt a touch lacklustre.)

Zelda: The Ocarina Of Time (1998: N64)

Arguably the best game ever made. The familiar world of Link and *Zelda* is given the N64 treatment—3D overhaul with new combat targeting—and the result is staggering. Luckily, and brilliantly, there are no dramatic changes to the familiar gameplay—save the shift from a birds eye view—it is a masterpiece, with a full and involving world full of small touches and brilliance that has yet to be rivalled.

Planescape Torment (1999: PC)

Very intellectual, but don't let that put you off this wonderful dark and involving RPG. More flexible than previous games based on the AD&D world, in that it lets you alter the main characters' alignment through moral choices taken all the way through the game. Multiple routes and endings mean that the experience can be quite different even with repeated play.

Grandia (1999: PlayStation)

A heart-warming RPG with a fantastic battle system. Don't let its child-like looks put you off. Though the plot is emotion-led and soppy it is a truly engaging and rewarding game. There are no random battles and the innovative battle system itself is one of the best around as a well-timed move can really throw your enemies off track. (The Dreamcast/PS2 sequel keeps up the great gameplay but doesn't have the same level of charm.)

EverQuest (1999: PC)

Sony's famous first attempt at a massively multiplayer online RPG. There is no set story as such—players log on (having to pay a monthly fee), and traverse an online fantasy world. Much of the game is statistic-heavy, and it sometimes feels like a chore to play, especially when you have to devote so much time to it. Conversely, the world is wondrous in its scope and detail, and once you've ingratiated yourself with the atmosphere, it soon becomes compulsive—so much so that critics have branded it 'EverCrack' due to its addictive nature.

Baldurs Gate 2 (2000: PC)

A superior AD&D game with outstanding depth and complex plot set in the Forgotten Realms. Create a new character or import one from the original *Baldurs Gate*, then immerse yourself in hundreds of hours of fun. The game is remarkably non-linear, particularly when compared to console RPGs; the ability to explore and pick and chose missions lets you feel as though you're creating your own story.

Shenmue (2000: Dreamcast)

Puts the 'role' in 'role playing' as you take control of Ryo, taking him through his day-to-day life as he investigates the death of his father. This is the game to shove in the faces of those nay-sayers that claim videogames can never be art; this remarkable game—sometimes under whelming, other times achingly profound—is another of those Very Unique Things that can only come from Sega. It is reason alone to buy a Dreamcast, and almost reason alone to be a gamer.

Phantasy Star Online (2000: Dreamcast)

As the title suggests, it's *Phantasy Star*, but online. Gameplay is extremely limited, and you may quickly tire of the repetitive combat and missions. However, the real fun comes in signing up to the Internet, ganging up with three friends and travelling to Ragol, unravelling mysteries and slaying monsters: it is the online aspect that makes the dynamic very special.

First Person Shooters

As the name suggests, the staples of this genre are a first person perspective and the use of projectile weapons. Often considered to be just PC-based, games using perspective and guns originated with funfair shooting ranges, which later evolved into indoor light gun arcade games and then light gun games for the home consoles. Following on from iD's groundbreaking work with *Wolfenstein 3D* and *Doom*, recent years have seen a flood of games with similar perspective dynamics, most utilising 3D engines. Most recently first person shooters for the home consoles have outdone the PC variants, but some of the earlier games are still classic examples of the genre.

Duck Hunt (1984: NES)

Taking arcade light gun fun into the home proved a good idea for Nintendo: this game was bundled with the NES and a lightgun and at the time offered basic but fun play.

Wolfenstein 3D (1992: PC)

iD's revolutionary and highly lauded first FPS, featuring the exploits of one rookie soldier taking on Nazi foes. Replaying today would highlight some inadequacies, but prolonged play and experimentation did reveal hidden rooms and weapons. Most importantly, however was the innovation of its graphics, using ray tracing and texturing to create the appearance of three-dimensional rooms.

Doom (1993: PC)

iD followed up *Wolfenstein* with a game that attempted to be gorier, scarier, and better. It succeeds on those counts, and while it seemed like more of the same for *Wolfenstein* fans, the impact of this release should not be understated. This was the game which made FPS as a choice genre, and the addition of networked functions allowing play between two computers cemented this as a future gaming function of choice.

Quake (1996: PC)

While *Doom* merely toyed with ray tracing and texturing, *Quake* (and, again, developer iD) revolutionised the genre with a specially designed game engine that generated its 3D world with polygons. The result was amazing, with fantastic graphics. The engine has since been adapted and used in countless other 3D FPS games. The game spawned two more sequels, and introduced the gaming community to fragging and rocket jumping. Also remarkable was the added opportunity for online play: log on via the Internet to fight with or against friends, family, and gamers around the world.

Time Crisis (1996: Arcade; 1997: PlayStation)

With its kidnap plot, fast moving 3D graphics and 2-player cooperative mode, *Time Crisis* was a huge draw in arcades—thanks to the large screens displaying the game, putting you in the midst of the action. While the camera is on rails, and there are common hazards (like civilians to avoid shooting), this is old-fashioned fun, almost matched by its PlayStation home version.

Golden Eye 007 (1997: N64)

It is a much-eulogised game, but it deserves it. One of the few FPSs that encourage stealth, thought and tactics rather than kill-em-all speed, this *James Bond* movie based game is the best example of a genre perfected. Yet one point is often overlooked: it's the only *Bond* game that doesn't feel the need to give you the obligatory missions using gadgetry and cars, etc., but still exudes *Bond*-ness. Everything is well balanced, from the controls to the content, and to this day it remains eminently playable.

Half Life (1998: PC)

Until this game, all other FPS used their first person perspective to its full only during the missions. Others had cutscenes and menus interspersed with the action, breaking any real continuity. *Half Life* runs completely from the perspective of Gordon Freeman, trapped in an accident at a scientific facility, having to fight his way out. There is never a break in the perspective, either—the game is continuous, save for minor loading between areas. Not as fun to revisit as *GoldenEye*, but the atmosphere and game engine makes for compelling, groundbreaking play.

Counter-Strike (2000: PC)

Terrorists fight against Counter-Terrorist paramilitaries in team-orientated play. The online functions mean gamers around the world have sleepless nights at their computers. Originally based on the *Half Life engine*, *CS* has grown to be an incredible game in its own right, offering a somewhat intense, exhilarating experience.

Police 24/7 (2001: Arcade)

The unique selling point of this arcade light gun game is that when you move, the perspective moves, thanks to motion sensors and cameras built into the arcade cabinet. It's a unique enough gimmick to make a very enjoyable experience that successfully attempts to push progress of the FPS/arcade light gun genre forward an inch. (Steer clear of the PS2 version, though; it is an awful conversion.)

Deus Ex (2000: PC)

One-quarter RPG, and one-quarter stealth game, but the rest is pure FPS. You play as JC Denton working for the government, helping combat terrorism, but discovering a vast conspiracy in the process. Each area allows multiple paths for play—sneakily enter a factory through the air conditioning ducts, or go in guns-a-blazin', for instance—sometimes the story changes based on how you play, and who you chose to trust. The content may not be entirely original—it owes much to other games in this and other genres, and also science fiction—but it is the unique and original presentation of these components that makes for such acclaimed gameplay.

Halo (2001: Xbox)

In all honestly, there is nothing truly original in *Halo*. Controversial words maybe, especially with this being the Xbox's 'killer app'. But what *Halo* offers is the most perfected of all FPSs. Every single area, weapon, vehicle, and enemy has obviously been refined until developers Bungie could push no further.

Strategy Games

Strategy is all about planning, and usually how to plan to best destroy the opposition during war. Strategy games can be in real time, requiring quick thinking and frenetic action, or turn-based, giving the player more opportunities to sit back and think things through. Resource management plays a great part, be it either managing money in order to construct objects or buildings or controlling materials to construct weapons. You must be constantly monitoring entire situations, gauging for moments of strength and weakness in an opponent, deciding what tactics and approaches to take in order to secure domination. In many ways the genre hasn't really evolved, as one of the earliest strategy series – Civilization – is still one of the best.

Civilization (1 onwards: 1991: PC)

One of the best strategy games ever? Almost certainly. Manage a civilization from scratch through turn-based play. Develop its cities, resources and industries, and try not to anger either the residents or other world leaders. A complex game that will leave you at your computer for hours, but suffers from imbalance; later turns in the game seem to take forever. Every edition is pretty good, and the series continues to remain ahead of the best of the strategy game.

Mega Lo Mania (1991: Amiga)

A decent strategy game which sorely needs a sequel. Play as one of four gods, and fight for ownership of various territories. You have to develop technologies, mine for resources, and produce weapons in order to succeed. Although the game was a little too short it had great charm, with memorable graphics, sound effects and some superb speech samples.

Cannon Fodder (1993: Amiga)

War has never been so much fun. Lead a small platoon of troops through a variety of missions, using strategic thinking or fire-like-crazy tactics to complete them. An accessible strategy game, with a dark sense of humour; proceedings are kept varied thanks to an array of weapons to blow the enemy apart with and differing terrains to traverse. The tiny sprites are pretty damn cool and die rather violently (if you like that sort of thing).

Worms (1995: PC)

Worms is a great multiplayer game for anyone who enjoys blowing up their friends over and over again. The game is filled with tiny adorable worms that you can take control of so that you can try and destroy a team ruled either by the computer or a friend. Mayhem ensues and everyone is happy. Except for single players who may feel the game lacks lastability.

Command And Conquer series (1995-Present: PC)

A real-time strategy game that spawned a million clones. Choose a side in an ongoing territory war and then destroy the enemy over a variety of missions that also require you to mine for spices and build factories and shelter. A compelling plot line holds everything together, in one of the few instances where full motion video sequences have passable performances, are quite engaging, and don't encroach on the otherwise flawless gameplay.

WarCraft II (1995: PC)

Playing as warlord of a fantasy empire your task is to manage a growing economy and other resources, all the while mounting an army to smash the opposition with. Great fun for fantasy fans—some elements are reminiscent of *Command and Conquer* but with orcs and daemons as troops—but with a great amount of variety, especially when playing multiplayer, where battles can be vast ordeals spanning multiple locations. Complicated yet very exciting.

Age of Empires 2 (1999: PC)

A classic real time strategy game that follows the evolution of the human race across hundreds of years. Charged with building up a globe-spanning empire from scratch, countless details are ate your disposal, and make you really care about the gaming world. Each civilisation has its style, leading to some brilliant designs and nice eye-candy.

Star Trek: Birth of the Federation (1999: PC)

Empire expanding space strategy at its best. Conquer the galaxy as the leader of either the Humans, Cardassians, Ferengi or Romulans. Diplomacy is generally a better option than straight out war here—most races have the same levels of distrust toward each other as shown on our TV screens. Graphics aren't out of this world though the slow but involving gameplay is. Similar to the also excellent Master of Orion games.

Shogun: Total War (2000: PC)

Control hundreds of soldiers in this fine strategy game set in feudal Japan. Follow campaign mode as you attempt to unite Japan under your flag or try out your skills in some actual historical battles. The 3D battle scenes are absolutely stunning and in battle terrain and the weather can be as important as the number of soldiers on your side.

Advance Wars (2001; Game Boy Advance)

Quality turn based strategy game for the portable generation. Typical strategy stuff, featuring army resource management but with a brilliant anime style. Featuring just the right level of detail, anyone can start playing and get seriously hooked by the punchy action. One of the must-have portable games.

God Games

God games are more a subcategory of strategy games, seeing as they require similar methods of resource management. Unlike strategy, they require you to aim for the growth of a home, city, business or civilisation, and follow a fairly linear progression towards large-scale management. Because of this, many run on their own distorted version of time that can be altered according to the needs of the player—if you don't want to sit around and wait for the yearly funds to increase, then sped up the action, or you need to stop and plan out buildings then slow down the time or pause the game entirely. Most important is the level of control handed to the player. The player is distanced from the main action, there are rarely single characters to control, instead they view everything from afar assessing when the time is right to up the price of living, or expand territory.

Little Computer People (1985: C64)

Before *The Sims* came this. A little man lives in a house with a dog. You can control some of his actions through the keyboard, but then you just sit back and watch him interact with his surroundings. He dances to music, plays on his computers, types letters to you and feeds the dog. Lovely.

Populous (1989: Amiga)

One of the first god games and still one of the best. You are a god who can manipulate your landscape and your followers. The followers are important because the more you have the more powerful you are. However, you are not the one and only deity around and you must defeat others, and their own followers in order to complete a map. The most recent *Populous* (*The Beginning*) is a rather different game, with a 3d perspective, and a Shaman rather than a god as the main character/player. It's all good though.

Sim City series (Original Version 1989, SimCity 2000 released 1993: PC)

The ultimate city-building game. Decide what areas of land should be commercial, industrial or residential, fine-tune the city's power and water needs, and build roads and landmarks. The level of detail within *Sim City* is overwhelming and is what makes the game so hard to switch off as you watch your newest city incident unfold. *2000* changed to an isometric view, with a larger map, suggesting an entirely new feel to the game.

Theme Park (1994: PC)

Hands up who wants to build a theme park! Starting with an empty plot of land, build rides, employ staff and hope the visitors enjoy themselves. Early versions of the game were a little bit too short and now the series has possibly been superseded by *Rollercoaster Tycoon*. However, this is still a decent game that's worth a look if you can get it cheap.

Rollercoaster Tycoon (1999: PC)

The game that beat *Theme Park* at its own theme. A strategy game with the basic premise of creating an amusement park that pulls in the visitors without running out of cash. A major draw was the variety of rides to fill your attraction with--there's more than just roller coasters on offer here (though they're damn good fun to build). Hours of roller coaster amusement.

The Sims (2000: PC)

Why play with a dolls house or be creative with Town Lego when you can play *The Sims?* Build a house from scratch or move a family into one of the pre-built homes. Although you don't get to see the Sims at work, you need to keep them happy and find them jobs so that they bring the cash in to buy the delightful home furnishings. After the initial house building any *Sims*-induced wonder can quickly dissipate, but the add-on packs keep the gameplay going that little bit longer. Visit the *Sims* website to download extra goodies.

Black and White (2001: PC)

Taking the word 'god' to its extreme, you are given a 3D world to look after, with the ability to cast miracles and move the earth. You also control a large animal, idol to the occupants of the land, who you use to perform your bidding. The choice to play benevolent or malevolent is down to you, and the world responds to your actions (regardless of their ethicality) suggesting that each player will have a slightly different experience. A hugely visionary game, it was unfortunately quite bugged upon release, but awe-inspiring nonetheless.

Flight Sim

Our flight simulation remit is considerably wider than what others may define it. The idea of allowing players to control airborne craft recurs in many games; some of them take this to an extreme with the 'sim', offering vastly complex environments and readouts full of dials and details. A majority of the games require weapons, and some form of dog fighting, but unlike shoot 'em ups, they are usually in limited supply, creating a more taxing level of resource management for the player. The shadow that science fiction casts over videogames has penetrated this genre quite heavily, with games creators taking the next step to offer fantastical flying arenas in outer space and in the skies of alien planets. The *Star Wars* licence, the *Wing Commander* games, and other series/franchises have taken the genre to a fantastical conclusion with vast empires and space dogfights that dismiss the rules of gravity at whim and allow for some of the most liberated play. But at the same time, other games, in their scope, use gravity, and their real world setting as the focus to rein you in (*Microsoft Flight Simulator* and *Pilotwings*, for instance). Either way, it is the freeform element that interests us—if it allows you the opportunity to zoom about the skies (or space) in almost any direction, then this is where you'll find it, regardless of the depth or complexity of control.

Elite (1984: BBC Micro; Spectrum)

A space exploration game placing you in the role of a space pirate/trader as you made a career for your exploits, working your way to becoming one of the Elite. Renowned for its near limitless possibilities—you were given a vast universe to travel around, and were able to travel and trade as you saw fit—the expansive world was a landmark for the time, and an influence can be felt in all space combat games following.

Mercenary (1986: C64)

Struggle to escape from a deserted planet after a crash-landing leaves you stranded. It's arguably a FPS, but most will remember the ability to fly craft and such over a vector rendered planet. Graphics were simple, but the storyline and dark sense of humour were not.

F/A-18 Interceptor (1988: Amiga)

More like an arcade game thanks to the accessible controls, this sim puts you in the pilot seat of the titular Interceptor and at the time offered unparalleled thrills. But the controls also featured easily mastered advance techniques. Hidden bonuses and an open-ended nature meant much time could be lost simply experimenting.

Wings (1990: Amiga)

You play as a First World War pilot who must complete a variety of missions such as dog fighting and bombing. Atmospheric—as you complete missions you read a pilot's diary involving you in the plot—with easy controls that make it immediately satisfying.

Wing Commander Series (1990-Present: PC)

Originally a fairly simple space combat game featuring flight-sim-lite (i.e. basic) controls, the series, following an ongoing intergalactic war, has since evolved into the territory of vast space opera. Later instalments are filled with video cutscenes, some of which starring science fiction stalwart actors (Mark Hamill, Malcolm McDowell), but these vast plotlines were coupled with great, if slightly restricted, gameplay.

Pilotwings (1991: SNES)

Covering a range of airborne events—skydiving, parachuting, etc.—as well as flying planes and helicopters, the notable feature for Pilotwings was a cartoony appearance merged with great physics effects. Particularly enjoyable are the stunts, and the ability to use a rocket-pack in later levels.

X-Wing (1993: PC)

The most engaging of the *Star Wars* games prior, which allows you to take control of various rebel craft. The key core is that it is not overwhelmingly *Star Wars*, it is more *Star Wars* by implication, thanks to the understated detail. Missions are entirely space based, so the only things you'll be able to crash into are other craft. Weapons and engines are controlled by a symbiotic energy management system, and the various campaigns and mission lead right up to the showdown against the Death Star.

TIE-Fighter (1994: PC)

The 'evil twin' of *X-Wing*, in which you get to play as an Imperial pilot, rather than 'rebel scum'. The plot is more dramatic and the gameplay has been made more immediate, which strangely suits the pared back controls the same way the leisurely pace of its predecessor did—the fact that both can use the same control mechanism yet can be used at different paces says much about the quality and effort that went into both titles. Missions and access to vehicles are better structured this time around, however, making for a more exhilarating, though not as immersive, experience than *X-Wing*.

Descent (1995: PC)

With a first person perspective putting you in control of a mining craft, your mission is to destroy the robots that have gone haywire. A good contrast of vast arenas and enclosed tunnels led to a cunning use of 3D engines and freeform movement.

Microsoft Flight Simulator series (1995-Present: PC)

As the name suggests, the games rely heavily on simulation. There are few game elements as such, given that the main core of the game is learning the countless processes and techniques in order to perform the perfect take off and landing, etc. With a wide range of craft to experiment with, it is lengthy play that makes the game satisfying; you'll be able to easily cope with environmental variants like turbulence and air traffic patterns once you master the controls.

Driving

Speed. To so many extents that is the core of this genre, in waging how fast you can move your vehicle. The genre seems split between realistic driving and kiddy cutenes, and each style has its advantages and benefits of either accurate detail or fantastically original game worlds. What compounds the driving core of speed is multiplayer participation—most of the games here can be played with two players and it is during head to head races with friends that the real hook of the genre appears, that of intense competition and sheer exhilaration.

Out Run (1986: Arcade)

Whether playing on the arcade or console version, *Out Run* was made special by its content. Instead of standard racing games, the aim is to beat another vehicle as it speeds along highways. The simple set up is complimented with some clever twists—there are multiple paths to follow in your attempts to beat your opponent—and some great attention to detail—you can even change the music that plays on the car radio.

Super Mario Kart (1992: SNES)

Mario and friends (and villains, too) go racing in this simple yet brilliant racing game. With a perfectly pitched control system and learning curve, very few racing games can compete with the fun *SMK* has to offer. N64 and GBA versions fail to completely capture the original magic. Computer controlled characters infamously cheat, but beating them makes the game all the more satisfying. The tracks give a brilliant tour of the *Super Mario* universe as seen in *Super Mario World*; powerups and weapons that litter the courses are a likewise inspired touch. A two-player battle mode based on the weapons makes for multiplayer magic.

Road Rash (1992: Mega Drive)

Motorbike racing with a twist—race other renegade riders around motor-ways, picking up weapons and attacking them as you zoom past. The original, while shallow and simplistic, fairs the best, as later versions generally seem quite poor.

Micromachines series (1994-present: Mega Drive)

Take control of a teeny-tiny little cars (based on the toys) and race around Land of the Giants-esque tracks; a kitchen worktop, a science lab, etc. The cars aren't always easy to control, especially at high speeds, but no one wants an easy ride. Sometimes frustrating, but always fun.

Ridge Racer (1995: PlayStation)

Shallow and by today's standards disappointing, but there was a reason why the game helped to sell so many PlayStations. The visuals no longer hold the magic they once did, but there is much variety within each track, and the range of cars quite impressive (although many of the good ones had to be unlocked via extended play).

Wipeout series (1995-Present: PlayStation)

While not our favourite of racers, the franchise has remained consistently popular thanks in part to its hyper-trendy soundtracks and graphical flare. A futuristic racer, that sometimes thinks it is faster than it really is, but is never-theless enjoyable thanks to some frenetic moments involving weapons and powerups that make sure the speed and action is constant.

Gran Turismo series (1997-Present: PlayStation)

Where the *GT* series excels is with its realism. Take your pick from hun-dreds of cars, from real life licences. So detailed is its world that it may be easy to complain, but the options allow so much variety and leeway that criti-cism may be churlish. Prolonged play leads to more satisfying driving, in one of the few instances where persistence really does mean you get better at the game.

Colin McRae Rally series (1997-Present: PC)

Intense realism from the *GT* mould, but this time in the form of skidding around muddier tracks. The great addition of co-driver adds to the atmosphere, and while the game is not as challenging as *Gran Turismo*, there are enough different play modes (especially in the later instalment) to keep you happy.

Burnout (2001: PlayStation2)

Frantic racing in the style of *Out Run*, but with a 128-bit sheen. Sort of *Gran Turismo*-lite, with arcade thrills thanks to the high speeds as you dodge through traffic on busy streets. Unoriginal, but with a compulsive charm. The computer-controlled characters have a tendency to cheat—enough to make *Super Mario Kart's* Luigi blush—but arguably it makes the experience more compelling as you zoom on towards the finish line.

Sport

Possibly the trickiest of genres to review, in that sports-based videogames are a mix of the natural and the unnatural. The games of the genre hold nothing on the sports they emulate, which are active compared to videogaming's relative laziness. Key presses and joystick twirling is not an accurate portrayal of the exertion performed by athletes, but in a strange twist this is certainly just as vigorous a way of making us mimic the actions of sportsmen. Realism is only partly necessary, and while the character animations constantly strive for realistic movement and style, the option to adjust things like weather and other variables in some games makes for a more controlled event, nothing like the real thing. We've avoided reviewing the licence based sports games that update every year, because while many are good, they offer little that is new to the genre.

Daley Thompson's Decathlon (1984: Spectrum)

In 1984 countless track and field games appeared trying to cash in on the popularity of the Olympics. Of them all, the *Daley Thompson* tie-in was the best, and is very much the epitome of 'button mashers'—sports games requiring you to frantically bash keys at speed as a substitute for running or similar activities. Graphical limitations aside the events had a manageable learning curve, gradually ranging from easy to difficult.

Speedball 2: Brutal Deluxe (1990: Amiga)

Not actually based on a real sport—the closest comparison is a cross between American Football and the fictitious sport from the movie *Roller-ball*—*Speedball 2* offered instant but subtle gameplay, fast action, and a sheen of wicked violence. Weapons and powerups are scattered throughout the arena to make for some frenetic fun. It improves upon the original by offering more play modes, making for a far more complete experience.

Sensible Soccer (1992: Amiga)

With a top down perspective, this is a quick and brilliant football game with depth. Using such tiny animations for the players was a masterstroke; the games can be fast and furious with so many players on screen, and the controls are very easy to handle making the game fun even for non-football fans. The game offered a great array of extras and options, and was completely customisable, meaning you could incorporate your favourite team or extra information.

Championship Manager series (1992-Present: PC)

Stats, stats and more stats are at the heart of this ever-popular football management game. Whether you want to manage your favourite team, or work your way up from the lower divisions, this is the game to play. Incredible detail means that you can become immersed in this game for several hours at a time as you search through available players to buy or minutely change the tactics and set up of your squad.

Tony Hawks Pro Skateboarder (1999: PlayStation)

Far from being a cheap cash-in on the back of Hawk's name, this is a varied skate game allowing you to pull off as many cool stunts as possible. Far easier to pick up than it looks, with impressive handling and a variety of skaters to utilise, all with basic moves and special tricks. The real pursuit becomes chasing after high scores and multiple combos—intensified when played as a race against a second player.

1080° Snowboarding (1998: N64)

An amazing looking game with a great soundtrack. The number of courses is limited at first (you unlock more as you complete certain goals), but the controls are perfect, capably using the analogue stick to balance weight and perfectly manage landings—no other snowboarding game comes as close to the level of tight control on offer. Jump and stunts are a lot of fun—almost anything you see can be pounced upon and slid across, down, or over—and the gravity is perfect, with the movement across the snow feeling weighty and realistic. The two-player mode is pretty dire, but that's a fair trade for such magic controls and atmosphere.

Jet Set Radio (2000: Dreamcast)

A skating game with a difference. The game revolves around the need to stop rival graffiti gangs tagging your territory, whilst not letting the cops attempt to stop your illegal activity. Skating is easy to get to grips with though some harder jumps will leave you screaming with frustration. Add the colour-ful cel-shaded graphics into the mix and you get a great (if not perfect) game, which is all too often overlooked.

Virtua Tennis 2 (2001: Dreamcast)

Improving the otherwise impeccable original *Virtua Tennis* is quite an achievement. The improvements are the addition of real-life tennis players, male and female (unlike the original's line up of all male made-up players), but also the addition of creating your own player. You can take your new char-acter through various tournaments, levelling up their statistics and improving their power and speed, etc. Like the original, the proceedings are held together with a simple and intuitive control system that never fails to let you down.

Pro Evolution Soccer (2001: PlayStation 2)

The moment this game appeared it was the football videogame of choice, despite a few flaws (rubbish commentary, and the better graphics have seen in other games). The reliance is on realism, and this is one of the few football games that rely more on tactical thought than simply chasing the ball around. The game really blossoms after hours of play, once you have mastery of some of the more complicated controls, and with finely honed skills two player matches are an odyssey to rival any pay-per-view match out there.

Beat 'Em Up

If there's one genre that has survived generation after generation of hardware, it's the beat 'em up. If you can't beat seven kinds of hell out of your best friend for real, why not do so in a virtual space? BEUs capitalise on the core of multiplayer gaming: competition. They take a great portion of their inspiration from martial arts with its controlled moves and attacks that consoles and computers dare to emulate. Many take slightly fantastical bents, with special moves, energy attacks, and combos that would make Jet Li feel inadequate.

Double Dragon (1987: Arcade)

Instead of arena based fighting, *Double Dragon* follows the story of two brothers having to battle through the mean streets of a city in order to rescue a kidnapped damsel. Offering both a single player and co-operative two-player mode, you have to walk the streets, battling thug after thug, culminating in a boss battle. Fighting was a touch rudimentary (there is one special move that is far too easy to rely on) but thanks to the large levels, some filled with tracks and obstacles, it was a lot of fun.

International Karate (1987: C64)

A superb game requiring you to fight karate champions on your progression towards a black belt rating. It may seem rudimentary now, but offers a range of realistic karate moves, spiced up with a free-for-all nature. Has since appeared on the Game Boy Colour and Advance where little has changed, although a tournament mode has been included.

Street Fighter 2 (1992: Arcade/SNES)

The most genre defining beat 'em up. Eight characters—each highly individual, almost iconic, with strengths and weaknesses and amazing special moves—battle for supremacy in various locations around the world. The first of the beat 'em ups with combos and special powers, mastering these lead to more depth than fighting games previously, and paved the way for the other gems of the genre that would emerge in later years. Those games may now have bettered *Street Fighter 2's* 2D graphics, but for any fighter fan this is their *Citizen Kane*.

Mortal Kombat (1992: Arcade)

Notoriously violent, featuring the common set-up—a variety of players fight to the death, using special moves and superpowers—with a slightly more realistic bent thanks to its over supply of blood and gore and photo-captured players. Finding the hidden fatality moves was fun; but as violence is the raison d'etre of the game, it never bested *Street Fighter 2*.

Virtua Fighter (1993: Arcade)

While content-wise the *Virtua Fighter* series has added little to the genre, it was the graphics that made it special, with the beat 'em up finally being shown off in a 3D environment. It took all the typical fighting moves, but the extra dimension for movement meant that players now had far more options when it came to dodging attacks and countering blows. Imperfect, but innovative.

Rival Schools series (1998: PlayStation)

While *Rival Schools* may offer nothing particularly new to the ardent fighter fan, there is depth an energy to it that keeps us constantly entertained. The premise is simple; rival gangs of school kids (and the occasional teacher) face off against each other. There are some terrific combos, a great tag player mode, and a heavy dose of anime action and humour.

Tekken 3 (1998: PlayStation)

More powerful-world-tournament-to-end-all-powerful-world-tournaments fun with the third iteration of the *Tekken* series. Out of all those released, *Tekken 3* stands out the most, giving its refinement of the character line-up (the previous two games' characters were too uneven and not individual enough) which is almost as striking as that of *Street Fighter 2*, although not as memorable.

Soul Calibur (1999: Dreamcast)

This beautiful mix of fist and weapon play makes for one of the most enjoyable beat 'em ups. It makes superb use of the Dreamcast's hardware, and has yet to be bested for quality and gameplay by any beat 'em up since.

Music/Rhythm Action Games

A fairly new genre, heavily influenced by Japanese culture, currently featuring only a handful of games compared to other gaming areas. The emphasis is on hitting keys in time to music, which are often pop-based tracks of all variety. Half the fun is derived from the peripherals available—some bordering on the outlandish—that aim to spice up the experience, with dance mats and controllers shaped like DJ equipment or instruments. The rest is pure bubblegum fun; great in multiplayer, often offering continued depth and some surprise challenges.

PaRappa the Rapper (1996: PlayStation)

The most rudimentary of all the music action games—you have to just match button presses with icons as they move across the screen—but the music, with brilliantly ridiculous rap lyrics, and animation make it very endearing.

BeatMania (1998: Arcade)

Play DJ with this great Konami game. The action is compounded with a brilliant mini turn-table/keyboard peripheral, and some great tracks (some original, some taken from pop tracks) make for a lot of fun. The peripheral makes for much of the enjoyment though—playing with a normal joypad gets a bit dull.

Vib Ribbon (1999: PlayStation)

A rabbit walks along a single white line that throbs in time to music and throws up loops and blocks that correspond the key presses—successful combinations mean the rabbit jumps across the screen without getting hurt. Timing is everything and the game can quickly become frustrating, yet it makes for good, if occasional, fun. For extended replay value you can use your own music collection and the white line will adapt itself to the music.

Dance Dance Revolution (1998-Present: Arcade)

As the name suggests, dancing is the core of the game here. While the arcade version features a large touch sensitive floor, marked with directional arrows for you to boogie on at certain moments, dance mats are available for the home version. Given the exceedingly active elements, it's great fun, especially with two dance mats, and while a lot of success relies on your own abilities, the variety of songs means it doesn't get boring.

Samba de Amigo (2000: Dreamcast)

What makes *Samba de Amigo* so much fun? Apart from the Sombrero-clad maracas-shaking on-screen dancing monkey? It has to be the controllers: two large red maracas are used instead of the joypad, and the notion completely changes the way you play. Gameplay consists of matching the actions of the monkey in the comfort of your own living room. The choice of songs can get irritating, but when playing with friends and grievances go right out the window (assuming you have a sense of rhythm, of course).

Space Channel 5 (2000: Dreamcast)

A musical version of Simon says, as you help space news reporter Ulala dance alien invaders to death. Great fun; another soundtrack success from Sega, and the retro-space design makes for great eye candy. A huge flaw however is the sometimes hit and miss controls—sometimes it registers when you have hit the rhythm, but other times not.

Rez (2001: Dreamcast)

Inspired by Kandinski and synasthesia, this on-rails shooter perfectly merges a trance soundtrack with twitch gaming, with shots and bombs creating musical riffs and beats. While the game is short, it is through repetition and trying to improve your score that the hidden joys of the game unfold. It is a game that can only be played to fully appreciate it. And, of course, the soundtrack is fab.

Puzzle Games

The real key to puzzle games is simplicity: it only takes one strong idea with one gameplay hook to offer hours of fun. A lot of these games have turned up on multiple platforms, often handheld, due to their accessible and brilliantly basic nature. Perhaps this is the genres all the tired other ones should look to for inspiration; while some of these games are unashamedly two-dimensional in what they offer, there is sometimes more inventiveness in one puzzle game than there is in, say, four average FPSs.

Marble Madness (1984: Arcade)

A slightly forerunner to *Super Monkey Ball*, that is simple, but deceptively so. The aim is to roll a marble around a track, using trackballs, avoiding obstacles, pitfalls, and enemies. A great test of dexterity and speed—your course was timed—painfully compulsive.

Tetris (1989: Game Boy)

Control blocks that fall from the sky. Flip the blocks to suit and drop them into lines across the screen to make them disappear. The blocks never stop coming as the speed and tension mounts. *Tetris* is pure addictive fun that doesn't need flashy graphics to be one of the best games ever.

Columns (1990: GameGear)

Columns of three coloured gems are dropped from the top of the puzzle area. You have to match up three gems of the same colour for them to disappear. Notable as Sega's answer to *Tetris*: it is in some ways more difficult than its Russian rival, and harder to master, but it's not quite as good, either, nor as deep. Persevere, though; like most puzzlers of a certain quality it becomes quite addictive.

Pipedream (1990: Game Boy)

Plumbing with no Mario or Luigi in sight. As water is pumped through an incomplete system of pipes you must lay out a series of connecting pipes making sure the water can flow. The game gets more complex as you progress, with faster flowing water, obstacles to plot around, and strangely shaped pipe pieces, with enough variety to ensure a compulsive game.

Lemmings (1991: Amiga)

Famous for its tiny graphics and mind-bending level designs. A group of lemmings must get from one end of a level to another. You can control their progress by assigning jobs to them – such as digger and builder. Of course you can also derive a lot of fun from this game by thinking up inventive ways to kill the lovely lemmings. The real beauty lies in the depth and variety of the tasks you could assign each lemming—this often leads to a wider scope of routes through each level. Add-on packs kept the fun going as the time went by, but a tricky 3D remake reached somewhat further than was really achievable by the premise.

Mr Driller (1999: Arcade)

Think *Tetris*, but in reverse. You control Mr Driller, and have to drill down through layers of multicoloured blocks that can either stick together or fall on you. Make it to the bottom without running out of air. Insanely addictive, with a very clever and simple design. While not quite as compulsive as *Tetris*, you will go back for more and more. If the blocks don't crush you first.

Chu-Chu Rocket (1999: Dreamcast)

A startlingly original puzzle game that doesn't involve fitting blocks together. Instead you must guide mice towards a rocket with only a limited amount of arrows to guide them. In multiplayer mayhem get as many mice into your rocket as possible and try and guide the mice-eating cats towards your enemies. Smart, simple, and compelling.

Super Monkey Ball (2001: Game Cube)

There's a monkey in a ball, and it is your task to tilt the floor to guide him to the goal. Simple, addictive, yet rarely frustrating; when it does frustrate, it is perversely enjoyable. The balance of single and two player modes is excellent; extra joy lies not only in the main feature, but six brilliant mini party games that are almost worthy of a game all of their own.

Culture

Games In Popular Culture

Despite what stereotypes say, videogames are not solely enjoyed by geeky males on the fringe of society. Videogaming is now a major part of culture, and shares elements with other media such as films and literature, but still remains unacknowledged, despite the fact that it clearly is popular.

The games industry has been growing steadily for some time now. Research supported by ELSPA (the European Leisure Software Publishers Association) showed that in the United Kingdom in 2000, more money was spent on leisure software (i.e. games) than the cinema box office (£943 million compared to £632 million). Also, the games industry is continuing to grow. For example, in the UK the games industry has grown by 111% since 1995; in contrast, video retail and cinema each grew by a third in the same period. The story is the same elsewhere in the world. For example, in the US, the Interactive Digital Software Association (IDSA) has reported that 60% of all Americans play video games (approximately 145 million people), and that the amount of games sold in 2001 had risen by 4.5% since 2000.

Games have been seen as entertainment for children and young teens for a long time. This is why so many newspapers report on children and the effects of videogames but ignore the fact that adults play too. Although children are still a valuable market for the videogame industry, a much wider range of people than this actually buy and play games. A Nielsen Media research study from 1999 showed that 74% of people using videogame systems were over the age of eighteen. 25% were aged 12-17, 40% were aged 18-34, and 34% were aged 35+. According to the IDSA, the average age of an interactive game player is 28. This does not deny the popularity of videogames amongst children, after all, at the time of the Nielsen survey teens comprised 10% of the population, cut still managed to be 25% of videogame players. Instead what this shows is that gaming is a major phenomenon amongst adults too.

This could be because older groups of the population have now more or less grown up with videogames. There are many people who view videogames as a relatively new phenomenon, yet there is also a surprisingly large section of society that can't remember life before videogames. When this group of people need something to do, they see gaming as a viable form of entertainment in exactly the same way they view film or literature.

So why else have videogames become as prominent as say film, when it comes to choosing how to be entertained? Another reason may be that videogames are particularly useful when socialising with friends. For example, take friends to a film and they can have a good time, but they can't interact with each other, while multi-player games with friends are all about interaction. The IDSA found out that 59% of most frequent game players play with friends. Apart from sports (which usually involves leaving the relative comfort of the home), there are few other forms of entertainment where friends can compete, have fun, and knock back a drink at the same time.

For decades aspects of gaming have been reflected in other media, such as film, television and literature. Games-related movies range from teen thriller *War Games* (computer whiz-kid ends up starting a nuclear power 'game' between America and Russia), to David Croenenberg's *Existenz* (about a virtual reality game). Games-lit (as opposed to chick-lit) includes such classics as Tad Williams's *Otherland* Quartet (evil men use children to create an online world), and Orson Scott Card's *Ender's Game* (young military recruits are trained in the art of war using computer games). There have been several television shows for gamers, all with varying degrees of success, and characters from television shows (like *The Simpsons* or *Spaced*) have demonstrated a preference for gaming. Sometimes games are so successful that they are made into movies (*Tomb Raider*, *Street Fighter*), or inspire them (*Final Fantasy*). This games-related-entertainment does not always result in quality end products, but they highlight this main point: that videogaming culture is huge and on par with any of the other media in popular entertainment.

In the same way that aspects of videogaming has bled into other media, the influence of films and literature can be felt in videogames. Videogames are, as their name suggests, a visual medium, closer to film than literature, yet to an extent both games, films and literature share one element: story.

'Story' is an account of incidents in their sequence or the order in which they occur. Nearly all games have a story, or a driving narrative. Part of getting the gamer to play is the introduction of a story, or the implication of a story; it gives the gamer a motive to play. A girl has been captured and must be rescued; the ultimate evil is trying to take over the world and must be stopped; different factions have landed on a planet but only one can survive, a football manager has limited funds to get his team to the top of the league, etc. Of course the gamer may well ignore all this, but that does not deny the existence of these stories.

The narrative in games suffers because of their interactive nature. The standard stories in books and films are fixed and the order of events within them unchangeable. Even with flashbacks and other devices, most narratives in films and literature are linear. Unfortunately the more linear something is, the less influence an outside force can have. Linear stories in games restrict the choices a gamer can make. It is impossible for any game to be completely linear, because the gamer would have no choices at all, and games that have come close to this just feel like interactive movies (*Dragon's Lair* for instance relied solely on moving a joystick to move from one scene to the next). This linearity might create a stronger story, but at the same time it creates a weaker game, where the gamer may feel he would be better off at the cinema with a box of popcorn.

Most games have a mixed amount of linearity. For example, gamers must take levels in a certain order, or complete one task before they can move on to another. Usually though, players can make various choices which suggest to them that their experience is unique because of their interaction. These choices may involve beating an opponent in a variety of ways or increasing a character's strength (or 'levelling up') before moving on to the next part of the story.

The *Final Fantasy* series is notorious for its high levels of linearity. This is particularly true at the beginning of the games (for example *Final Fantasy VII*), where a couple of hours may be spent setting up the story, while all the player can do is move the character(s) from point A to point B. Usually at this point the gamer has to read lots of text, and is told what buttons to press. Throughout the game the player can make several choices that give a feeling of true interactivity: who to put on their team, what villages to visit, what level to train up to etc. At the same time, there are many game areas that can only be visited once certain tasks have been completed. However, if a group of say, *Final Fantasy VII* players, got together, they would probably soon realise that their gaming experiences had all been remarkably similar—the game's driving narrative would not be different, only the way the game was played from one narrative cue to another. There is nothing really wrong with this, except the realisation that the story was always going to outweigh individual decisions.

Linearity can be explored in various ways in videogames. *Deus Ex* has a fairly linear structure, but manages to have non-linear gameplay. For instance, certain tasks can be completed in a variety of ways using different types of approaches: stealth or action are two typical options, and computer controlled characters will react accordingly. Also, the central character in *Deus Ex* is customisable: players can change his abilities as time progresses, and these abilities mean they will find easier paths to navigate through levels that they had not been allowed access to previously. Thus the gamer has the framework of the overall story coupled with the extra changes affected by their own choices. *Baldurs Gate*, a role-playing game on the PC, does participation and linearity slightly differently. A complex story is set up, but the game area is huge, and the player is rarely restricted or told what they can visit when (this in part is because the game is on the PC and thus has access to lots of memory). While new players may find it easy to accidentally wander into difficult areas, the level of involvement and the scope for experimentation is high.

Primarily, of course, games are fun. They can be bright, colourful, funny, fast, dark, or mysterious. Players enjoy engaging with them as they can be highly atmospheric and a lot of fun to interact with. To many gamers participation will seem to improve the in-game story, as their actions will appear to be vital to the plot. People cannot experience this sort of participation in the same way through film and literature, although you could argue that the imagination required while reading a novel works in a similar way.

Videogames are still evolving. This is why it's still possible to argue that games may not be comparable to film and literature, why they aren't considered works of art, why some people think there's never been a truly impressive story set within a game. This is why videogames sometimes attract so much criticism. But we are still at the beginning of a new form of entertainment. Things can only get better.

Branding Versus Gameplay

In videogaming, branding is big business, but if you ask the average gamer how big branding is in their gaming life they may well just shrug. Yet brands are huge in the gaming industry; if a game is successful there is a great chance is will spawn a sequel and merchandise turning it into a franchise of its own. Furthermore, there are many computer games made solely on the back of licences acquired from sources outside of videogaming, like sports and film. There are also company brands, or logos for certain machines, with some companies using famous game characters as mascots. All these brands play on the same thing—selling a specific kind of experience, using advertising and the iconography of the associated licence or product.

There are many series, characters and licences that have spawned countless games, sequels and reinventions. Think *Star Wars*, *Star Trek*, *Final Fantasy*, *Tomb Raider*, *The Sims*, *Monkey Island*, *Fifa*, *Tony Hawks*, *Pokémon*, *Mario* and *Sonic*. These kind of games account for a hefty proportion of the total game revenue worldwide; the *Pokémon* franchise has sold over 50 million games worldwide. The *Final Fantasy* series is similarly successful and by November 2001, the series had achieved global sales of 33 million. ELSPA reported that in 2000, licence-based games accounted for 45 per cent of the all-formats UK top 100 videogames chart, with official sports bodies and sports stars being prominent in most of these titles.

Licences are an easy way to get the attention of the public. Most licences are quite successful despite not always being of particularly high quality either in gameplay or originality. Parents and kids who don't read games reviews but stumble into a games shop are likely to buy based on what they are familiar with, and this previous knowledge tends to be other aspects of popular culture such as film and television. Many football games are updated each year, and while this is to allow the addition of new players and the general revision of team and league information it also has the handy advantage of being an almost guaranteed cash-cow year after year. As with football clubs that bring out expensive strips too often, the 'real' football fan and gamer will feel obliged to keep up to date with the latest game.

Star Wars and *Star Trek*, the two very well know science-fiction series that have spawned vast ranges of merchandise, have a large library of tie-in videogames. These games do not stick to a specific genre like sports games, instead various different genres are explored in different games, and they just happen to include elements from the show/films. Thus, this kind of licenced game has much more freedom than other licences as it can be applied to any genre of game—sometimes the resultant games can be highly acclaimed or innovative, but at others they can feel like mindless cash-ins. Therefore the life of the brand and the potential money derived from it is almost unlimited as long as the licence remains popular and the games made are not of a dire quality.

It is a somewhat overly cynical view to say that branded or licenced games are nearly always of a poor quality—just because something is popular doesn't mean it is bad. The *Final Fantasy* games had been averagely successful in the US previously, but only after the release of the seventh instalment did the worldwide gaming industry sit up and take notice. Each individual *Final Fantasy* game is usually quite good, but it is the amazing power of the *FF* brand that gives developers Square confidence enough to release sequel after sequel. They have even released many *Final Fantasy*-related games which do not directly link into the series such as the various spin-offs featuring 'chocobo' (a birdlike creature that appears in many of the games).

Publishers and developers also use scant updates as a way of securing the strength of their brands. *The Sims* has sold millions of copies worldwide and is well known for capturing the imagination of a broader gaming audience than usual. It did this through the elements of play that allow gamers to easily identify the game with day-to-day life. *The Sims* has been out since 2000, but despite its popularity no sequel has yet been released. Instead add-on packs have been coming out with alarming regularity. Each supplementary pack is close to the price of a full game, yet requires the original game to run—for a *Sims* fan to get the complete experience they are likely to end up paying for the equivalent of three or four full price games. *The Sims* is a fairly entertaining game, but can get repetitive. It feels as if the only concern that games publishers really have regarding the gamer's wallet is that money is leaving it and paying for their games.

The first *Tomb Raider* was an excellent action adventure game featuring the ultimate male fantasy figure Lara Croft. The game has spawned several sequels, but Ms Croft is a very strong brand in her own right, having graced magazine covers and being used to advertise the drink Lucozade. If there is any problem at all with the glut of sequels, it is that there lies a danger of producing a game that is little different to the one before it; the sequels to *Tomb Raider* are uninspiring, feeling more like repetitions of the original, just with new levels and slightly better graphics. Such sequels lack originality and create easy money for those behind the scenes. A further worry is that game developers and publishers who know that they can make x amounts of money from producing a sequel to game y, will have little incentive to invest time and effort in an unproved game or format.

Of course originality in games does not necessarily matter. As already discussed, sequels are particularly prone to unoriginality, but this does not always mean that a game will be of poor quality. In burgeoning franchises there are many sequels that are in fact superior to the game that generated them. For example *Command and Conquer: Red Alert* is perceived by many fans of the series to be much better than the original, and Nintendo's *Mario* games tend to improve with each instalment.

Consider how much these brands have permeated popular culture. Sony, Nintendo, Sega and so on can all afford to make spin-offs and tie-in toys and products for their most successful games. You can buy *Final Fantasy* figurines, *Mario* soft toys, and endless *Pokémon* merchandise; you can walk into a bookstore and buy a *Resident Evil* novel; you can buy DVDs of a Street Fighter cartoon.

What of the companies that make the machines that play these franchises? In many cases characters become synonymous with a manufacturer, and these mascots are championed as the reason to own a machine. For example, Mario will forever be associated with Nintendo—and each Nintendo console features at least one Mario game. As Nintendo own the rights to Mario, he will not appear on any non-Nintendo format; you will have to buy a GameCube or a Game Boy to play a Mario game. The same goes for *Pokémon*, which is closely identified with the Game Boy platform as well as Nintendo, and previously this also applied to Sonic the Hedgehog who acted as Sega's exclusive mascot and rival to Mario in the 16-bit heyday.

The story is quite different for Sony, who since the launch of the PlayStation has not aligned itself too closely with characters or games that are solely championed as the need to own their device. There is no figurehead for Sony the lifestyle brand. Eschewing the Mario/Sonic route taken by Nintendo and Sega, Sony's blank slate nature of their console has worked in it's favour—players are allowed to associate whatever they want with the device, be it sports games, 3D platformers, or RPGs.

The brand of the hardware company (Microsoft, Nintendo, Sony etc) is just as important as the games released for them, and they can have an incredible influence on the games buyer. Though many people will still buy a machine based on the games that it can play, and the quality and reputation of those games, the image of the console does influence purchase. Often people are looking for an entertainment system as much as a games machine. Although Nintendo is sticking to its all-about-games guns for the moment, both Microsoft and Sony have produced machines that play music and films, vying for a place in the market to rival standard stereos or DVD players. In fact during the Japanese launch of the PS2 more consumers bought the machine to play DVD movies on than PS2 games, showing that Sony may be more reliant on selling a lifestyle accessory (like their walkmans) than a machine that hinges on specific titles.

Unfortunately the identity of the companies behind the machines can have a negative effect on the brand. Nintendo's GameCube and Game Boy are often written off as machines 'for the kids'; Sony's PlayStation is for 'the mass-market with no taste'; and the Xbox is a 'PC-clone from money-hungry Microsoft'. From this it is clear that sometimes the brand can work against the company. Consequently some are making an attempt to move away from the brand, or rather the old image, and create a new one instead. For example Microsoft is very keen to emphasize the individuality of the Xbox and their name can only be found in the small prints of advertisements. Nintendo are trying to shake their tame image by featuring more games with mature content. However, even when an image has negative connotations it can benefit the company by creating niches for them to work in. Thus, it isn't a huge problem for Nintendo that a lot of children end up with their machines—the more users, the better. Similarly, Sony is happy with the incredibly large mass-market, and Microsoft doesn't mind starting off with attracting the more 'hardcore' gamers.

So, in this age of *No Logo* ethics, it is clear that branding and franchises exist to a great extent in videogaming. While the common conception that anything using the weight of a brand to sell is in fact inferior may be partly justified, this isn't always true. As is always the case with videogaming, it is the perceived quality of the games that matter, and it is up to the gamer to find this quality, and the games producers to supply it, regardless of licence or label.

Joystick Envy: Women In Gaming

Since there have been games there have been women playing games. Fact.

The IDSA (Interactive Digital Software Association in the US) reported that 43% of people who play interactive games are women. ELSPA's (European Leisure Software Publishers Association) annual report showed that the games available via Sky Digital's set top boxes attract a playing audience that is 44% female. The IDSA also found that 49% of game purchasers are women (although presumably some are buying for others, e.g. male children). Unfortunately games developers and their publicists do not appear to notice this. Or at least this is how it seems. All too often articles appear on the lack of women playing games or how surprising it is that women play games. There are also debates on what can be done to encourage more female game players into the fray. Of course it is often slightly frustrating to women that the industry is so surprised that women play its games.

To say that female characters are not present in games would be wrong, but the portrayal of them remains a touch wanting. Women do feature in a large proportion of games, often quite out-of-proportion physically. Games that feature a large ensemble cast of characters do tend to have a female presence, and other genres feature women protagonists occasionally. Unfortunately in ensemble games the women seem more to serve as 'token' characters, rather than characters in their own right or at the centre of the action. It seems as if these women are only there to placate complaints, and show that the female sex is equal in the gaming world, but when there are fifteen characters, twelve of which are male, there is hardly an equal division of the sexes.

A game in which a female character is the protagonist (or at least among the main characters) usually has several problems. One which becomes particularly grating is clothing. It is not that believable that women racing or on an adventure, for example, would be happy wearing only a bikini – but it happens again and again in games. Teeny-tiny clothes seem to be extremely fashionable in the universe's that certain games inhabit.

Female characters such as Lara Croft (from *Tomb Raider*) would at first glance seem to create a positive role for women in the videogames industry. The *Tomb Raider* games have been phenomenally successful, particularly in Europe and the US. Lara is a strong independent woman, adept at solving puzzles and an action hero to boot. These are all good things. She also has a remarkably curvaceous figure that is shown off in every frame of the game. Some women do have great bodies. However, Lara's is a little unrealistic. She has been designed not to be a believable character, but to be a male fantasy. Men enjoy playing as her, but more women would enjoy playing as Lara if she was a realistic representation of womankind. Regrettably, it also suggests that if she wasn't so attractive, the game would have fewer players—women are not allowed to be remotely unattractive, for fear that male gamers will be put off. This may well be true, but this shouldn't encourage the use of ridiculously shaped women in games, instead it should encourage better gameplay.

Women often surface in games without being playable characters. They are also represented through plot. The motive to play in some games is because a female character needs help somehow. It is possible to argue that this just encourages altruistic behaviour in players, both inside and outside of the gaming world. In reality it just gives women a bad name. Male characters embark on amazing adventures and defeat evil foes in terrible circumstances. If they get trapped they fight their way out. Female characters on the whole seem to get captured and languish. Princess Peach rots in Bowser's castle until Mario rescues her; where's her fighting spirit? Plot and motive for gamers to play is important and arguably necessary, but it is frustrating and unoriginal that these plots revolve around women in peril so often.

It is not fair to say that women are always depicted in a negative light in games. For example, in the NES game *Metroid* the character Samus shows strength, agility and other positive action-based qualities, and also wears suitable clothing for such tasks (all-over armour). She is only revealed at the end of the game to be a woman. But did it have to be such a 'surprise' that Samus was female, i.e. does *Metroid* challenge the gamer into questioning the assumption that only males succeed, or does it assert the assumption that it is 'surprising' for a woman to act in such a way? Also, a lot of the perceivable good points are detracted by the replay option that allowed you to play with the character in little or no clothes.

Should there be games made specifically for the female gamer? There are games aimed specifically at girls available but they tend to be aimed at pre-teen girls—never at women—and cover patronising topics such as fashion and boys. Many games are quite successful, more so in the US, where the girl games industry is a particularly lucrative one. The major producer of girl games in the US, is Mattel, which makes the games based on their Barbie dolls (including the likes of *Barbie Fashion Designer*). In 1999, Mattel dominated 65% of the girl games market. Purple Moon was an independent company, averagely successful compared to Mattel, which made girl games. Purple Moon tried to move away from fashion-orientated girl games; their *Rockett* series was about relationship-building and other issues at Junior High. Unfortunately the company folded in 1999 due to increased consolidation in the videogames market, with Mattel's share on the rise. Then, rather ironically, it was bought by Mattel a month later. HerInteractive is a newer company that makes software based on the books about Nancy Drew, the female teenage detective. These games involve mysteries and problem solving, which at least moves towards giving girls a bit more credit than the fashion games also available.

There is a market for girl games; obviously if there was not such a viable market then Mattel would not waste money producing them. There is nothing wrong with young girls liking these games of course (championing the cause of women gamers does not include putting any restrictions on what girls can play), though it is a pity that they aren't introduced to other sorts of games as well. It is a shame however, that these games aren't always of the highest quality, and are so often lacking in depth or variety. Yet even the success of girl games does not prove that younger females who play games actually want these games—parents will be responsible for many of the purchases, buying into the supply that the publishers have set up. Nor does this address the fact that if developers do think it is worthwhile targeting games at girls, why don't they make any games specifically for women.

What do women and girls want from games? It is often suggested (usually by men, or women who don't play games), that women are bored by masculine games. That they find the violence within them pointless, and would much rather be playing passive games about relationships, for example. This opinion can border on the offensive. After all, would male gamers like to be told that some of the games available to them were 'typically male'? Genres that are perceived to be dominated by masculinity include fighting games, first person shooters, or racing. Where does this leave role-playing games, or god games such as *Sim City*? Are the men who play these games emasculated? Is there something wrong with women who want to play *Quake*? No. Women are not bored by games that are action-packed, suspenseful, and generally fun and violence is not pointless in all games - usually it is placed in the context of a game as a means necessary to save oneself.

Women want the same from games as men. Again, like men, within a female games playing population there will be many variations in the type of player. Housewives who play *The Sims* because it allegedly reminds them of daily life are just as valuable female game players as young women who love running around *Phantasy Star Online's* planet Ragol, slaying monsters.

Perhaps the problem with women and the games industry is that girls are not 'told' that game playing is okay. Games are marketed towards men, hence the voluptuous nature of characters like Lara Croft—the exact same practice is used when marketing male dominated games magazines. Boys are steered by society, from an early age, into becoming more attuned and relaxed towards technology than girls and so have easier access to games in the first place. If there are differences in what girls and boys want or expect out of games, it is because of nurture, not nature.

Women are represented in various ways in the gaming world. Whether it is as the maiden in distress, sexy protagonist, or token character, women are at least visible in games, if not satisfyingly so. However, the one strong area where games are aimed specifically at females is the pre-teen market in the US, and these are generally throwaway games. More time should be spent encouraging women to play any sort of game, and more characters should be represented as extraordinary ordinary women. Women are not the only minority in the games industry; people with disabilities, or people of different races may also find it hard to seek adequate representation and support within the games industry. Perhaps the situation would be improved further if more women, and more minorities, worked within the games industry, for developers and games publishers. In time, as more females grow up with games around them, the situation may improve somewhat on its own.

Killer Instinct: Violence In Gaming

Picture the scene. A school somewhere on the planet. In this school a young person does something violent. Maybe murderous. The incident makes the news. Somewhere along the line, in the media's reporting of this, videogames get mentioned as a pastime enjoyed by those responsible for the crime. It gets outlandishly implied from this that videogames were of course somehow responsible for causing the event. This description may sound trite, but according to some sectors of the media, videogames are very bad. They're violent and evil and can only cause trouble.

Violence is defined as 'physical force applied to the intent of causing harm or damage.' There is no denying that videogames contain violence: from the outlandish explosions of *Space Invaders*, through to the jumping on the heads of enemies in *Mario*, to the sniper action in *Deus Ex*. All of these games (and a majority of others) feature varying elements that require the player to control a character who must proceed through arenas/levels/locations using any means necessary. More often than not, this means extends to violence of some form. A common thought extracts from this that the players of these games are invariably encouraged, through this exposure to violence, to act violently outside of gaming. Videogames get blanketed in a negative light, and their redeeming features are forgotten. But do videogames encourage violence? And how do they really affect gamers?

Mortal Kombat is a notoriously violent fighting game, released in 1992. Not particularly unusual, but it did have some standout differences to its competitors. The characters were very realistic, with action and movement captured from models and actors; most notably the game absolutely teemed with violence. While any fighting game cannot avoid violence, *Mortal Kombat* went over the top in its attempts to be gory. The game was more famous for its gruesome deaths and fatality moves, when a player could perform acts on an opponent such as pulling out the spinal cord, or ripping the heart out of the chest. The game created uproar across the globe. In the UK questions about *Mortal Kombat* were raised in Parliament. In America it went as far as the Senate, where it was marked out (along with other games) as a prime example of a game that could lead to crime and violence. Sega came under attack for hosting a home console version on the Sega Genesis/Mega Drive. Nintendo escaped much of the furore because *Mortal Kombat* was sanitised on the SNES; the blood and fatality moves had been removed. However, this did not please players, and in the end the Sega version of the game far outsold the SNES game. But the gorier aspects of the game could only be unlocked with continued, expert play of the game or special combinations or button presses.

All this political discussion about violent games resulted in the creation of a ratings system for games in the US.

Hence games are rated by various bodies, by ELSPA and the BBFC in Europe and the UK and by the ESRB in the US. This is supposed to restrict access of the most violent and disturbing games to adults only. Of course ratings on games are not necessarily going to be effective (because of shops who sell to under-age players, or parents who buy on the behalf of their children), but they at can at least show the amount of adult games readily available. Looking at the amount of games rated as suitable only for over-eighteens, it becomes apparent that although a lot of games may have an element of violence in them (such as making opponents 'faint' in *Pokémon*), only a very small minority are generally considered to be 'adult only'. Less than 1% of games are rated 18 by ELSPA or the BBFC rating systems, and in the US the ESRB (Entertainment Software Rating Board) found that only two of the top-selling games of 2001 were rated for 'Mature' audiences. This can be attributed to the fact that many games are bought for children by parents or non-games players as gifts, plus children would not be allowed to buy the games with mature content. However, when the average age of a game player is 28, it is clear that the market for adult gamers is huge, but the fact that only a fraction of successful games are classed 'mature' shows that games do not have to be adult-themed to appeal.

It cannot be denied however, that there is the occasional game that may overstep the mark, featuring too much violence. One recent game that may fit into that category is *Hooligans*, a game about loutish football fans. The object of the game is to successfully control a group of hooligans, whose favourite team is in the Euro-league. The gamer must then complete various missions such as breaking into a football stadium, or eliminating the opposition. Enemies include not only the opposing teams, but also the police. The group can visit brothels, pubs, dope shops and gun shops. The game is likely to be unsuccessful but this is due not to the senseless violence but the fact that the game is generally thought to be of very low quality. Therefore, violent games are not successful because they are violent, but because they have other redeeming features too, such as actually being fun to play. Pointlessly violent games such as this sometimes struggle to find support within the games industry - *Hooligans* could not find distribution by an ELSPA (European Leisure Software Publishers Association) member in the UK.

Games don't always influence people to behave badly. Otherwise the 145 million Americans who play videogames would include a far higher proportion of people who had committed various crimes and misdemeanours. Out of all the people who have committed crimes and were then revealed to have played videogames at one time or another, it is highly likely that nearly all of said people will have also watched television (as most console games require the use of a television set to play). How then can anyone decide that playing videogames is more likely to trigger violence than watching television?

Some people may argue that it is the active participation in videogames that increases their negative influence. During a game it is usually up to the player to select when violent acts occur and who they are committed against. There is rarely any moral system applied save for that implemented by the gamer themselves, and this tends to be where the blame against the violence in videogames often arises from. However, other aspects of popular culture that frequently influence gamers may depict violent acts too. Television is not interactive but it shows real-life as well as fictional violence, thus blurring the boundaries between them. Who then can say which form of entertainment is more damaging? After all, no game can be 100% realistic and so mature game players should be able to see a clear line between gaming and reality.

Perhaps, then, the problem lies more with individual people who may happen to play games, rather than the violence within games. If someone is ready to stand up and fire real bullets at real people, can we really blame a game they played? Can the same logic that leads us to denounce the likes of *Doom* also allow us to blame *Risk* and *Cluedo*? Can we not also argue that the perpetrator of the violent act may have acted even if they had not been possibly influenced by a videogame?

Regardless of whether or not videogames encourage violence, many games also have redeeming features that can result in positive attributes for the player. It is a common joke that children often argue that platform jumping can help hand-eye coordination, so that they have a reason for playing so many videogames. The UK government education and technology agency BECTA carried out trials in schools to investigate aspects of computer games that could aid learning. They discovered that *The Sims* and *Sim City* (both effectively world-building/resource management games) helped with student's ICT skills such as multi-tasking and problem solving. *Championship Manager*, a data-heavy football management game, resulted in increased interest in databases. Accordingly, it would seem that at the very least there are some games capable of producing positive qualities in students. Other games teach valuable lessons about the number of approaches that can be made in any situation. *Metal Gear Solid*, the successful stealth game, requires the gamer to walk around levels where many guards will attack the character Solid Snake on sight. The player can kill the guards, but they are also given the option of using stealth to get around them. The game is frequently easier this way, and thus the player is rewarded for negating the option of violence and choosing more passive means.

If games are too violent, or are in any way for responsible for violence in the real world, then what can be done to stop this? Unfortunately any restrictions on games, either on the violence within them, or on the people who buy them (for example the age ratings), are unlikely to be entirely successful. There are always ways to get around such things. In any case it is likely that gamers who are predisposed to violence and violent entertainment would simply turn to violence in other forms. This is a long shot, but it's possible that unable to get what they wanted through a fictional medium, such players would have an increased likelihood of committing violent acts in the real world.

Sadly the people trying to curb violence in videogames sometimes go too far. *Advance Wars*, a classic turn based strategy game for the Game Boy Advance, was delayed in Europe because of the September 11 attacks. It was a war game, no doubt about it. However, it was not a game that in any way supported terrorism, and was one among hundreds of war games readily available across the gaming industry. Also, while the game was unavailable in the UK, it was still available to buy in the US.

There are many violent hobbies enjoyed throughout the world including martial arts, and other physical sports, and participants in these are never seriously warned against the possibly detrimental effects their hobbies may have on their behaviour in the 'real world'. There is not yet a clear and definite link between playing violent videogames and committing serious violent acts away from them, it is more mindless hyperbole by a media looking for a scapegoat.

Resources

Books

The Revolutionaries at Sony by Reiji Asakura, McGraw-Hill Education, 2000, 0071355871, £12.99

The Rough Guide to Videogaming by Kate Berens and Geoff Howard, Rough Guides, 2001, 1858287855, £6.00

Supercade edited by Van Burnham, MIT Press, 2001, 0262024926, $49.95

From Barbie to Mortal Kombat edited by Justine Cassell and Henry Jenkins, MIT Press, 1998, 0262531682, £12.95

High Score! by Rusel Demari and Johnny L. Wilson, McGraw-Hill Education, 2002, 0072224282, £18.99

Re:Play by Liz Faber, Lucien King Publishing, 1998, 1856691403, £19.95

Die Gestalten Verlag, 2000, 3931126447, £25.99

The Effects of Video Games on Children: The Myth Unmasked by Barrie Gunter, Sheffield Academic Press, 1998, 1850758336, £12.95

Joystick Nation by J.C. Herz, Abacus, 1997, 0349107238, £9.99

The Ultimate History of Video Games by Steven L. Kent, Prima Lifestyles, 2002, 0761536434, $14.99

Game On edited by Lucien King, Lawrence King Publishering, 2002, 185669304X, £19.95

Playing for Profit by Alice LaPlante and Rich Seidner, John Wiley & Sons.,1999, 0471296147, $29.95

A Brief History of Tomorrow by Jonathan Margolis, Bloomsbury, 2001, 0747553351, £8.99

Sony: The Private Life by John Nathan, HarperCollins Business, 1999, 0006530915, £8.99

Trigger Happy by Stephen Poole, Fourth Estate, 2001, 1841151211, £7.99

Arcade Fever by John Sellers, Running Press, 2001, 0762409371, £12.99

Game Over by David Sheff, GamePress, 1999, 09669617096, $19.95

The Essential Guide to Videogames, Carlton Books, 2001, 1842223798, £17.99

Sega Arcade History, Enter Brain! Press, 2002, 4757707908, ¥1800

Sega Consumer History, Enter Brain! Press, 2002, 4757707894, ¥1900

Websites

Microsoft: www.xbox.com

Nintendo:

   US: www.nintendo.com;

   Japan: www.nintendo.co.jp;

   Europe: www.nintendo-europe.com

Sega:

   US: www.sega.com;

   Japan: www.sega.co.jp;

   Europe: www.sega-europe.com

Sony:

   UK: www.uk.playstation.com;

   USA: www.playstation.com;

   Japan: www.jp.playstation.com

IDSA: www.idsa.com

ELSPA: www.elspa.com

Blessed Magazine: www.blessedmagazine.com

Atari Age: www.atariage.com

Atari History Historical Society: www.atart-history.com

Nintendo Database: www.classicgaming.com/nindb/

GameFAQs: www.gamefaqs.com

Joystick 101: www.joystick101.org

Game Research: www.game-research.com

Gamasutra: www.gamasutra.com

Gamespress: www.gamespress.com

The Essential Library: History Best-Sellers

Build up your library with new titles published every month

Conspiracy Theories by Robin Ramsay, £3.99

Do you think *The X-Files* is fiction? That Elvis is dead? That the US actually went to the moon? And don't know that the ruling elite did a deal with the extra-terrestrials after the Roswell crash in 1947... At one time, you could blame the world's troubles on the Masons or the Illuminati, or the Jews, or One Worlders, or the Great Communist Conspiracy. Now we also have the alien-US elite conspiracy, or the alien shape-shifting reptile conspiracy to worry about - and there are books to prove it as well! This book tries to sort out the handful of wheat from the choking clouds of intellectual chaff. For among the nonsensical Conspiracy Theory rubbish currently proliferating on the Internet, there are important nuggets of real research about real conspiracies waiting to be mined.

The Rise Of New Labour by Robin Ramsay, £3.99

The rise of New Labour? How did that happen? As everybody knows, Labour messed up the economy in the 1970s, went too far to the left, became 'unelectable' and let Mrs Thatcher in. After three General Election defeats Labour modernised, abandoned the left and had successive landslide victories in 1997 and 2001.

That's the story they print in newspapers. The only problem is...the real story of the rise of New Labour is more complex, and it involves the British and American intelligence services, the Israelis and elite management groups like the Bilderbergers.

Robin Ramsay untangles the myths and shows how it really happened that Gordon Brown sank gratefully into the arms of the bankers, Labour took on board the agenda of the City of London, and that nice Mr Blair embraced his role as the last dribble of Thatcherism down the leg of British politics.

UFOs by Neil Nixon, £3.99

UFOs and Aliens have been reported throughout recorded time. Reports of UFO incidents vary from lights in the sky to abductions. The details are frequently terrifying, always baffling and occasionally hilarious. This book includes the best known cases, the most incredible stories and the answers that explain them. There are astounding and cautionary tales which suggest that the answers we seek may be found in the least likely places.

The Essential Library: Currently Available

Film Directors:

Woody Allen (2nd)	Tim Burton	Ang Lee
Jane Campion*	John Carpenter	Joel & Ethan Coen (2nd)
Jackie Chan	Steven Soderbergh	Clint Eastwood
David Cronenberg	Terry Gilliam*	Michael Mann
Alfred Hitchcock (2nd)	Krzysztof Kieslowski*	Roman Polanski
Stanley Kubrick (2nd)	Sergio Leone	Oliver Stone
David Lynch (2nd)	Brian De Palma*	George Lucas
Sam Peckinpah*	Ridley Scott (2nd)	James Cameron
Orson Welles (2nd)	Billy Wilder	Roger Corman
Steven Spielberg	Mike Hodges	Spike Lee
Hal Hartley		

Film Genres:

Blaxploitation Films	Bollywood	French New Wave
Horror Films	Spaghetti Westerns	Vietnam War Movies
Slasher Movies	Film Noir	Hammer Films
Vampire Films*	Heroic Bloodshed*	Carry On Films
German Expressionist Films		

Film Subjects:

Laurel & Hardy	Marx Brothers	Film Music
Steve McQueen*	Marilyn Monroe	The Oscars® (2nd)
Filming On A Microbudget	Bruce Lee	Writing A Screenplay
Film Studies		

Music:

The Madchester Scene	Beastie Boys	Jethro Tull
How To Succeed In The Music Business		The Beatles

Literature:

Cyberpunk	Philip K Dick	The Beat Generation
Agatha Christie	Sherlock Holmes	Noir Fiction
Terry Pratchett	Hitchhiker's Guide (2nd)	Alan Moore
William Shakespeare	Creative Writing	Tintin
Georges Simenon	Robert Crumb	

Ideas:

Conspiracy Theories	Nietzsche	UFOs
Feminism	Freud & Psychoanalysis	Bisexuality

History:

Alchemy & Alchemists	The Crusades	The Black Death
Jack The Ripper	The Rise Of New Labour	Ancient Greece
American Civil War	American Indian Wars	Witchcraft
Globalisation	Who Shot JFK?	Videogaming
Classic Radio Comedy	Nuclear Paranoia	

Miscellaneous:

Stock Market Essentials	How To Succeed As A Sports Agent	Doctor Who

Available at bookstores or send a cheque (payable to 'Oldcastle Books') to: **Pocket Essentials (Dept VG), P O Box 394, Harpenden, Herts, AL5 1XJ, UK**. £3.99 each (£2.99 if marked with an *). For each book add 50p(UK)/£1 (elsewhere) postage & packing